THE MERCHANT
OF VENICE

EDITED BY

H. L. WITHERS

FORMERLY PROFESSOR OF EDUCATION, THE VICTORIA UNIVERSITY OF
MANCHESTER; SOMETIME SCHOLAR OF BALLIOL COLLEGE

BLACKIE & SON LIMITED
LONDON AND GLASGOW

BLACKIE & SON LIMITED
5 Fitzhardinge Street,
London, W.1
Bishopbriggs, Glasgow
BLACKIE & SON (INDIA) LIMITED
103/5 Fort Street, Bombay

Printed in Great Britain by Blackie & Son, Ltd., Glasgow

PREFATORY NOTE

I have been allowed, by the indulgence of the General Editor and of the Publishers of 'The Warwick Shakespeare', to follow a method of arrangement somewhat different from that pursued in other volumes of the series. I have aimed at concentrating attention, in the first instance, on the Play itself, its plot, and the persons who were concerned in it. It is meant that a reading of the whole Play, as nearly continuously as possible, should precede any use of introduction or notes. Wherever practicable, the learner is himself to verify comment or criticism. To this end, blanks, between brackets, have often been left to be filled in after requisite search for the passage referred to. The Appendix on Prosody presupposes that the Play is being constantly read aloud or repeated, and that metrical exercises are being attempted in Blank Verse. It is taken for granted that a few very well-known books are within easy reach—a 'Globe' edition of Shakespeare, Professor Dowden's *Primer*, Dr. Abbott's *Shakespearian Grammar*, Professor Skeat's *Etymological Dictionary*, and, if possible, the Variorum Edition (edited by by Dr. H. H. Furness) of *The Merchant of Venice*; and, further, that these books are actually handled in course of study, both in preparation and in school-work.

All this, I am aware, gives a rudimentary look to the volume. But *The Merchant of Venice* is often the first of the plays to be taken up in detail, and at the outset of advanced Shakespearean study everything depends on a stirring of the learner's own interest and activity, and the formation of sound habits of work. So he becomes fitted to make proper use of a more erudite commentary.

H. L. W.

THE WARWICK SHAKESPEARE. General editor, Professor C. H. HERFORD, Litt.D., F.B.A.

Play	Edited by
ANTONY AND CLEOPATRA.	A. E. Morgan, M.A., and W. Sherard Vines, M.A.
AS YOU LIKE IT.	J. C. Smith, M.A., B.A.
CORIOLANUS.	Sir Edmund K. Chambers, K.B.E., C.B., M.A., D.Litt.
CYMBELINE.	A. J. Wyatt, M.A.
HAMLET.	Sir Edmund K. Chambers.
HENRY THE FOURTH—Part I.	F. W. Moorman, B.A., Ph.D.
HENRY THE FOURTH—Part II.	C. H. Herford, Litt.D., F.B.A.
HENRY THE FIFTH.	G. C. Moore Smith, D.Litt., Ph.D., LL.D.
JULIUS CÆSAR.	Arthur D. Innes, M.A.
KING JOHN.	G. C. Moore Smith.
KING LEAR.	D. Nichol Smith.
LOVE'S LABOUR'S LOST.	A. E. Morgan, M.A., and W. Sherard Vines, M.A.
MACBETH.	Sir Edmund K. Chambers.
THE MERCHANT OF VENICE.	H. L. Withers.
A MIDSUMMER-NIGHT'S DREAM.	Sir Edmund K. Chambers.
MUCH ADO ABOUT NOTHING.	J. C. Smith, M.A., B.A.
OTHELLO.	C. H. Herford, Litt.D., F.B.A.
RICHARD THE SECOND.	C. H. Herford.
RICHARD THE THIRD.	Sir George Macdonald, K.C.B., D.Litt., LL.D.
ROMEO AND JULIET.	J. E. Crofts, B.Litt.
THE TEMPEST.	F. S. Boas, M.A., LL.D.
TWELFTH NIGHT.	Arthur D. Innes, M.A.
THE WINTER'S TALE.	C. H. Herford.

CONTENTS

ADDENDUM: SHAKESPEARE'S STAGE IN ITS BEARING UPON HIS DRAMA, by Prof. C. H. HERFORD. Litt.D

INTRODUCTION.

I. THE PLOT.

In the days when Venice was the busiest and wealthiest city in all Europe, there lived in it a rich merchant named Antonio, who by means of several great ships of his own traded eastward as far as India, and westward as far as Mexico. This Antonio, at a time when all his wealth was at sea, wishing to furnish his young kinsman and dearest friend, a soldier and scholar called Bassanio, with means to pay his court to Portia, a lady of Belmont in Italy, borrowed the sum of three thousand ducats, for three months, from an enemy of his own, one Shylock, a Jew, on agreement that, if he failed to repay the sum in time, he should suffer the loss of a pound of his own flesh. On the selfsame night in which Bassanio, thus equipped, set sail from Venice, an acquaintance of his, by name Lorenzo, fled to the mainland of Italy with Jessica, Shylock's only child, carrying off also a quantity of his jewels and money. This loss so inflamed the Jew's malice, that when Antonio's ships failed to come home within the period of three months, Shylock flung him into prison and clamoured to the Duke for execution of the forfeit on his bond. Meantime Bassanio, by a right choice among three caskets respectively of gold, silver, and lead, having won Portia to wife, in the very hour of marriage heard of Antonio's danger, and, provided by Portia with three times the sum needed, sped to Venice. His intervention failing, Antonio was saved in extremity by Portia herself, who, in the guise of a Doctor of Civil Law, followed her husband into the Duke's Court of Justice. The trial over, they returned severally to

Belmont, Bassanio taking Antonio with him; there Portia, by means of a ring which in her disguise she had got from Bassanio, made clear to him who it was that had delivered his friend from death.

2. SOURCES OF THE PLOT.

Note.—This section is only for pupils who can read, or get somebody to read to them, at least a few extracts either from the authorities given below or from the abridgment in Furness' Variorum Edition. For others it will be unintelligible and useless.

1. Shakespeare did not as a rule invent the incidents which occur in his plays, but borrowed them, in outline at least, from Shakespeare's very various sources. Some of his plots are plots not original. founded on older plays, others on romances; several are taken from Sir Thomas North's version of a French rendering of *Plutarch's Lives.* Scholars have spent endless pains in tracking out the old plays and stories on which Shakespeare drew for material; a number of them were collected and published in the year 1843 by John Payne Collier, under the title of *Shakespeare's Library.*

2. In the case of *The Merchant of Venice,* the outline of the plot, as has been given above, was found by Capell as one of a collection of stories in an Italian book called Main outline of *Il Pecorone,* written by a certain Ser Giovanni Merchant of Venice derived Fiorentino, and printed in 1378. A modern from *Il Pecorone.* translation of it is given in the second volume of Collier's *Shakespeare's Library;* but no translation of Shakespeare's time has been discovered, and either such a translation once existed and has since perished, or else Shakespeare read the story in the original Italian. [For another possible alternative, see § 4, below.]

The story in *Il Pecorone* is, in main particulars, the same as that given above. We find in it a Venetian merchant fondly devoted to a young kinsman, and this kinsman in love with a fair and wise lady of Belmont, who is only to be won by the suitor who shall undergo successfully an extraordinary test; we have the same pledge with a Jew, made for the same purpose, followed by the lover's success and the merchant's bankruptcy, and later on by a trial in which the merchant's rescue is achieved, through just the same interpretation of the law, by the lady in the same disguise; and finally, on their return to Belmont it is by means of a ring, begged from her husband when in Venice, that she is able, after due banter and mystification, to prove her identity with the unknown lawyer.

There are minor differences: for instance, in the Italian story none of the names of persons are the same as Shakespeare's. The lover makes *three* voyages to Belmont; the sum borrowed is *ten* thousand ducats; when the marriage takes place the young kinsman forgets the merchant, and is only accidentally reminded of him just as the time allowed by the bond is on the point of expiring; and so on.

But, besides these slight variations, two important differences in incident are made by Shakespeare. First, he changes the method by which the Lady of Belmont is to be won, from its unsuitable form in *Il Pecorone* to that of the choice among three caskets; and secondly, he gives the Jew a daughter, whose elopement with a Christian forms an important part of the play.

3. The sources of these two variations must be looked for elsewhere. (i) The story of a choice among three vessels, respectively of gold, silver, and lead, with inscriptions somewhat similar to those in the play, and with a marriage depending on the right choice, occurs in the *Gesta Romanorum*, a Latin collection of mediæval tales, made in England probably about the thirteenth century. This collection was translated into English, became extremely popular, and was frequently printed in Shakespeare's time.[1] (ii) A story resembling in some points that of Jessica has been found in the Tales of Massuccio di Salerno, who flourished about 1470.

Sources of the main changes of incident.

4. Scholars have proved that both the story of the Pound of Flesh, and the story of the Caskets, were widely popular, and that they occur in slightly different forms again and

---

[1] Any good library will possess the reprint of this collection, published by the Early English Text Society.

again in European and in Oriental literature.[1] But it is certain, from accumulation of coincidences, that

Conjectured in-
fluence of an old
play called The
Jew.

it was upon *Il Pecorone* and the *Gesta Roman-*
orum that Shakespeare drew for the plot of the
Merchant of Venice. It has been conjectured,
indeed, that Shakespeare did not use these sources at first
hand, but that the two stories had already been combined to
form a single play, and that it was this play that Shakespeare
used as his material. This conjecture is founded on a reference which has been discovered in a book called *The Schoole*
of Abuse, published in 1579, written by a certain Stephen
Gosson, a student of Oxford. The book is an attack on the
poets and playwrights of the time, and among the plays
specially excepted from blame by the author is " *The Jew* . . .
shown at the Bull . . . representing the greedinesse of worldly
chusers and bloody mindes of usurers". This description is
exceedingly short, but it is certainly apt enough if it refers
to the combined tales of the Bond and the Caskets.

Two other possible references to this play of *The Jew* have
been discovered : one in a letter of Edmund Spenser's, written about 1579, and another in a play called *The Three Ladies*
of London, printed in 1584. These two references are, however, both slight and doubtful, and since not a line of the
play itself survives, the conjecture that Shakespeare founded
The Merchant of Venice upon it must remain conjecture only,
though an extremely probable one. Even granting its truth,
we only set *Il Pecorone* and the *Gesta Romanorum* one step
further back in the pedigree of the plot, for that they are in
the direct line of its ancestry cannot be doubted.

5. So far we have been dealing with the sources of the
incidents only. Shakespeare owes nothing of his character-
drawing to *Il Pecorone* or the *Gesta*. These

Possible proto-
types of Shylock.

old tales are tales of incident almost entirely,
and the persons who take part in them are but slightly out-
lined, as slightly indeed as we find the characters in the
Arabian Nights, the most famous of all collections of the kind.

---

[1] For details, refer to F. S. Boas, *Shakspere and his Predecessors* (Murray,
London, 1896), page 215, note.

(a) As to the character of Shylock, it has been supposed that its germ is to be found in Christopher Marlowe's play *The Jew of Malta*, which was written about 1589 or 1590. It is agreed that Shakespeare owed much in a general way to Marlowe, and particularly in versification. It is quite certain that Shakespeare knew his *Jew of Malta*, an exceedingly popular play, repeatedly acted about the time when *The Merchant of Venice* was produced. Principal Ward, in his *History of English Dramatic Literature*, has collected a number of parallels between the two plays, to which may be added one that he does not notice. [See note on iii. 2. 239.]

Marlowe's Barabas.

But all the resemblances added together do not make the debt of Shakespeare in this case more than a very slight one. The stories of the two plays are completely different; and between the characters of Barabas of Malta and Shylock of Venice,—once granted that each is a Jew and a usurer, that each lives by the shore of the Mediterranean, and that each has an only daughter who is converted to Christianity,— there is only so far a parallel that they may be said never to meet. Charles Lamb has put the difference between them thus:

"Shylock, in the midst of his savage purpose, is a man. His motives, feelings, resentments, have something human in them. 'If you wrong us, shall we not revenge?' Barabas is a mere monster, brought in with a large painted nose to please the rabble. He kills in sport, poisons whole nunneries, invents infernal machines. He is just such exhibition as, a century or two earlier, might have been played before the Londoners by the Royal Command, when a general pillage and massacre of the Hebrews had been resolved on by the Cabinet."

(b) One other source of possible suggestion to Shakespeare must be mentioned. It had long been supposed that, except by travelling, Shakespeare could not have had any personal knowledge of Jews, since they had been banished from England in 1290, and did not receive formal permission to return until the time of

Dr. Roderigo Lopez.

the Commonwealth. It has been proved, however, by Mr. S. L. Lee,[1] that Jews did find their way into England in Tudor times, and that in particular one named Lopez was for some twenty years, towards the latter end of the sixteenth century, a prominent figure in London and at Court. He was one of the first physicians of his day, and had the Earl of Leicester and, later, the Queen among his patients. In 1594 he was hanged at Tyburn on the charge of conspiring with the King of Spain to poison, first, a Portuguese pretender named *Antonio,* and secondly—as was alleged—Queen Elizabeth herself. The history of Dr. Lopez must have been well known to Shakespeare, and may possibly have suggested other points besides the name of his enemy, Antonio.

6. To recapitulate: the main outline of the incidents of the play is taken from one of Ser Giovanni's tales in *Il Pecorone,* with two main changes, a substitution

Recapitulation.

and an addition. The substitution occurs in the nature of the test by which the Lady of Belmont was to be won: this, namely the choice among three caskets, Shakespeare took from the *Gesta Romanorum.* The addition, the story of the Jew's daughter and her elopement, may be paralleled in a few points from a story of Massuccio di Salerno.

Lastly, while it is certain that in drawing the figure of Shylock, Shakespeare had in his mind—if only by way of contrast—Marlowe's *Barabas,* it is also established that he may very well have had personal, first-hand acquaintance with Jews in his own country.

3. CONSTRUCTION OF THE PLOT.

Content as Shakespeare was to take the main outline of his story from romances already existing, he was careful so to shape it in detail that it should work in with the temper and the motives of living men and women.

With him, a story was

> "just a stuff
> To try the soul's strength on, educe the man".

[1] In *The Gentleman's Magazine,* Feb., 1880.

But in pitting his heroes and heroines against circumstance, he brought circumstance into relation with them and their surroundings. Improbable, for example, as a string of bare incidents, the story of the Pound of Flesh becomes manifestly true in relation to Shylock and Antonio. In the play, the bond appears no longer as a chance contract between strangers, but as a plan for revenge imposed by one bitter enemy on another in the guise of a 'merry sport', which, in the nature of the case, will never come to serious execution. The Christian merchant, fresh from denouncing interest, cannot draw back from a bond in which—to please him—no mention of interest is made. Moreover, he had only just pledged 'his purse, his person, his extremest means' to his dearest friend to help him to win the heroine of the caskets; generosity, therefore, will not allow him to hesitate. Finally, the Jew's ferocity in afterwards exacting forfeit is made comprehensible by the loss of his daughter and his ducats. With such wonderful skill has this part of the story been handled, that readers are finally almost divided in sympathy between Antonio and his would-be murderer.

Modifications of the stories of the Bond,

The riddle of the caskets is similarly humanized. It becomes part of a scheme designed by a dying father for the protection of an only child, a girl of incomparable beauty, heiress to great riches. So formidable, therefore, are the conditions imposed, that all but the most earnest suitors are repelled from even an attempt at the enterprise (i. 2. 107), and, over and above the father's inspired assurance (i. 2. 26) that it would never be solved by anyone who did not 'rightly love', the lottery constitutes a real test of insight and devotion.

And of the Caskets.

The stories of the Bond and the Caskets, thus transformed, are most artfully interwoven throughout (compare i. 2. 100; ii. 8. 39; ii. 9. 100), and at one point with notable skill. In *Il Pecorone*, as mentioned above, the successful suitor forgets his merchant friend for some time after marriage; but Shakespeare makes the bad news from Venice arrive before the wedding, so that the Trial of

Blending of these two stories.

the Caskets is, as it were, carried on into the Trial of the Bond, and Bassanio and Portia are not fully man and wife until after they have rescued the friend whose devotion had made their union possible.

Shakespeare's introduction into the play of yet a third story,—the Elopement of the Miser's Daughter,—far from *The Third Tale,* unduly complicating the plot, serves to knit *that of the Miser's* together more closely its different events and *Daughter.* characters. Shylock is thereby brought into fresh relations with Antonio and his friends. Even Launcelot the clown is no unimportant link in the action. As servant first to the Jew and then to Bassanio, as go-between for Lorenzo and Jessica, and finally by his appearance at Belmont, he passes from one group to another, and makes a fantastic cross-thread in the embroidery of the plot. So dependent are the three stories upon one another—from the first scene, in which they are all set going, to the last, in which they are all combined and concluded—that if Antonio had not signed the bond, Bassanio could not have gone a-wooing; if Bassanio had not won Portia, there would have been no one to save Antonio; if Lorenzo and Jessica had not wandered to Belmont, Portia could not so readily have quitted Belmont for Venice.

It is by this vital interdependence of feelings and fortunes among the persons of the Drama, not by any abstract idea *The 'unity of* or moral common to all the parts, that 'unity *action' in the* of action' is secured by Shakespeare. A useful *Plot.* mechanical help to a study of the method by which Shakespeare interlaces the various threads of interest in the play, is to make a list of the scenes, entering opposite each the place where it is laid, and the persons who take part in it. Inspection of such a list will show that the action passes constantly from Belmont to Venice and back again. By these transitions the different 'intrigues' of the plot are kept moving, and, further, the effect of lapse of time is produced. *Management of* duced. It is one of the cleverest points in the *time and place.* stage-craft of the play, that the formidable period of three months is made to pass, and is felt to be passing,

and yet we are nowhere conscious of a gap in the action.[1]
This result is produced, as was pointed out by Professor
Wilson in reference to *Othello*, by the use of 'double time'.
That is to say, phrases implying short spaces of time in the
future, are combined with others implying long spaces of time
in the past, in such a way that both the continuity and the
lapse of time are kept before our minds. Thus from i. 1. 70
and i. 3. 166 we should gather that Bassanio is to meet Lorenzo
and Shylock again the same day; but from Jessica's words in
iii. 2. 281 ff., and indeed from the very circumstances of the
case, it is clear that a long interval must have elapsed between
Acts i. and ii. So, again, from the last few lines of ii. 2.
one would suppose that the farewell feast before Bassanio's
departure is referred to, and that he starts that night; yet, a
little while before (line 104), he had said "put these liveries
to making", a matter requiring some time. No sooner has
Bassanio started than the indications of the lapse of time
become more frequent ("Let good Antonio look he keep his
day", ii. 8. 25) ("Yet it lives there unchecked that", &c.,
iii. 1. 2), and from line 83 in the last-mentioned scene we
learn that Tubal has been from Venice to Genoa and back
since Jessica's flight; so that we are quite prepared to find
that on the day of Bassanio's choice among the caskets he
receives news that the bond is already forfeit. Yet, when
we come to inquire minutely how and where Bassanio had
spent the three months, we find—as we deserve—that the
inquiry is futile. It is important, at the outset, to recognize
that some lines of Shakespeare study lead to nothing; and
to grasp the reason of their failure. They assume that the
poet worked in a spirit which was, as a matter of fact, foreign
to him. For the purposes of a play, matters of time and
place are stage-properties of the same kind as paste-board
crowns and paper trees. To make them 'real' in minute
detail is to make everything round them false, just as to put
a 'real' ring on the finger of a painted portrait destroys the
truth of the picture.

[1] Vide Furness' brilliant note on 'Double Time', as used in this play and in the
'Agamemnon' of Æschylus. Variorum Ed., 1892, pages 338 to 345.

Thus, to ask where Belmont precisely was, is to put a question which has no answer. Shakespeare has no further localized Belmont than to put it on the mainland of Italy, apparently on the sea-coast, at no great distance from Venice on one side and Padua on the other.

It is enough for a play that its indications of time and place should 'semblably cohere'. *The Merchant of Venice* will repay endless study as a piece of dramatic construction, not from any attempt which it contains at historical or geographical 'realism', nor from any symmetrical formula connecting its several parts, but from the perfect lucidity with which it sets forth how, at a crisis of their fate, a number of people became involved with one another, how they severally bore themselves, and how by the action of each the fortune of all was determined.

4. THE PERSONS OF THE PLAY.

Thoroughly to enjoy Shakespeare, it is necessary to become intimate with the people of his plays. Intimacy is impossible at second-hand; it must be gained for one's self and gradually, with Shakespeare's people as with others, by seeing what they do, by hearing them talk, and by noting what their neighbours feel and say about them; in a word, by living with them for a while. After the first reading of a play has given an understanding of its main outlines, it is well to take the chief persons separately, and to observe—

(i) The precise share which so and so has in the action.

(ii) Sayings of his which seem to tell most about him.

(iii) Any noticeable opinions of him expressed by enemy or friend.

After bringing, in this fashion, our own notions to a point, we can enjoy the views of critics and commentators. A great delight waiting to reward anyone who will in this way make a careful analysis of *The Merchant of Venice*, is the reading of Mrs. Jameson's study of 'Portia' in her *Characteristics of Women*, and of Hazlitt's view of 'Shylock' in his *Characters of Shakespeare's Plays*.

The following notes on the various characters of the play are not intended to supersede the student's own analysis, but to be read after such an analysis has been made, for the purpose of comparison. Where a blank has been left between brackets, the student is meant to fill in the reference to act, scene, and line, for himself.

1. (a) SHYLOCK was 'old' (iv. 1. 168) at the time of the events which made him famous. We know a good deal of his history. He had wandered, in the way of his *His history and* trade, as far north as Frankfort [   ], *position in Venice.* but settled at Venice, whose laws, liberal as times went towards aliens, enabled him to follow his business securely. He had only one child, a daughter, called Jessica; his wife, Leah, must have died soon after the child's birth, for, while Shylock remembered her fondly, and treasured a ring she had given him when he was a bachelor [   ], Jessica never speaks in a way that suggests she had known her mother. Jessica kept house for her father with the help of a single servant, in a style—forced on her by Shylock—of the severest simplicity.

By trade he was a 'usurer', that is, he lent money out at interest. He had acquired great wealth, partly by knowledge of his business and of the commercial position of those with whom he dealt (i. 3), partly—as his enemies asserted—by taking advantage of his clients' weaknesses and mercilessly 'selling them up' if they were unpunctual in payment (iii. 3. 22). Devoted as he was to money-making, his race and his religion occupied quite as much of his thoughts. The Jews in Shakespeare's Venice were allowed a synagogue to worship in [   ]; they were obliged to wear a distinctive dress, and, no doubt, lived (both by their own choice and by compulsion) in a quarter of their own. They were granted unusual privileges before the law: the Duke himself went in pursuit of Lorenzo and Jessica at Shylock's bidding [   ], and it was again the Duke in full court who would not wrest the law against the foreigner. But in matters of ordinary intercourse they had to endure, even at the hands of the noblest among the Christians, the bitterest

contempt and most intolerable personal insult [   ].
To this Shylock[1] replied with a hatred all the fiercer for being
concealed, and with an exclusiveness all the haughtier that
he found himself despised by men whom he regarded as his
inferiors in religion and in race. Shylock regarded his nation
as 'sacred' [   ], and greatly esteemed his tribe;
in imagination he was constantly back in Palestine, with
the folk of his sacred Scriptures. He quotes Jacob, whose
'wise mother' [   ] gave him his position among
the patriarchs, as an example of heaven-prospered trading;
his servant he thinks of as the offspring of Hagar; pork
reminds him of the conjuring of the prophet of Nazareth; in
his enemy he sees a resemblance to the 'publicans' who
had vexed the souls of his countrymen sixteen centuries
before; his very oaths ("by Jacob's staff", "by our holy Sabbath", "cursed be my tribe") speak of his people and his
faith.

(b) How ought we to feel towards Shylock? The vast
difference of opinion on the point is reflected in the diverse
interpretations of the character which have held
the stage. In the last century Macklin laid
stress upon his 'snarling malignity', and presented a frightful figure of devilish cunning and
hatred—a combination of mere miser and murderer—which
is described as follows by a spectator. "The first words
which he utters are spoken slowly and deliberately: 'Three
thousand ducats'. The *th* and *s* twice occurring, and the
last *s* after the *t* have a lickerish sound from Macklin's lips,
as if he were tasting the ducats and all that they can buy;
this speech creates for the man, upon his first appearance,
a prepossession which is sustained throughout. Three such
words, thus spoken, and at the very first, reveal a whole character. In the scene in which he first misses his daughter he
appears hatless, with hair all flying, some of it standing up
straight, a hand's-breadth high, just as if it had been lifted

*Conflicting inter-
pretations of his
character by ac-
tors and critics.*

---

[1] A poem of Browning's is often a most helpful commentary to a play of Shakespeare's. To understand Shylock better, read Browning's *Holy Cross Day*, and
Filippo Baldinucci.

up by a breeze from the gallows. Both hands are doubled up, and his gestures are quick and convulsive. To see a man thus moved, who had been hitherto a calm determined villain, is fearful." [1]

On the other hand, in this century, Kean and Irving have followed out that view of his character which is summed up in Hazlitt's fine phrase: "He seems the depositary of the vengeance of his race". This view, extended so far as to make Shylock a martyr, has been wonderfully expressed by Heine (a Jew himself) in a superb criticism of the play, translated on pages 449–452 of Furness' Variorum Edition. A few sentences from it are given here. (Heine is visiting Venice.) "I looked round everywhere on the Rialto to see if I could find Shylock. I found him nowhere on the Rialto, and I determined to seek my old acquaintance in the synagogue. The Jews were just then celebrating their Day of Atonement, and they stood enveloped in their white talars, with uncanny motions of the head, looking almost like an assemblage of ghosts. There the poor Jews had stood, fasting and praying from earliest morning; since the evening before, they had taken neither food nor drink. Although I looked all round the synagogue, I nowhere discovered the face of Shylock. But towards evening, when, according to the Jewish faith, the gates of heaven are shut, and no prayer can then obtain admittance, I heard a voice, with a ripple of tears that were never wept by eyes. It was a sob that could come only from a breast that held in it all the martyrdom which, for eighteen centuries, had been borne by a whole tortured people. It was the death-rattle of a soul sinking down dead-tired at heaven's gates. And I seemed to know the voice, and I felt that I had heard it long ago, when in utter despair it moaned out, then as now, 'Jessica, my girl!'"

(c) Thus actors and critics differ as to the proportion in which hatred and pity and fear should be blended in our feelings towards Shylock. One error we must guard against from the first, that, namely, of supposing that Shakespeare meant

---

[1] Quoted, p. 374 of Furness' Variorum Edition, from a letter written in 1775 by Lichtenberg, a German visitor to England.

either to attack or to defend the Jews as a nation in the

The point of view for sound judgment. person of Shylock. Writing 'with a purpose[1]', in this narrow sense, is not in his spirit. A Jew came into the story, and Shakespeare has taken care that we should understand both him and those with whom he dealt. With modern Englishmen, among whom Jews take a foremost place for public spirit and gener-osity, the difficulty is not so much to be fair to Shylock as to conceive the feelings with which Antonio regarded him.

(*d*) To do so we must follow carefully the indications which

Causes of hatred towards Jews. Shakespeare gives us. Shylock was hated for four main reasons—his pride of race, his religious opinions, his mean and shabby habit of life, and his way of doing business.

1. As regards the first point, it is clear that the refusal of Jews in the middle ages to eat and drink with Christians, and

Their racial exclusiveness. their abhorrence of intermarriage with them, were not only bitterly resented, but further laid Jews open to horrible suspicions. The penalty for seclusion of life is unrefuted calumny.[2] The ghastly legend of St. Hugh of Lincoln was spread in various forms all over Europe, and in some parts is still believed. And even where the hatred for a people who kept so strictly apart did not take so hideous a shape, it appears in the not unnatural belief that Jews were an unkind[3] and uncharitable race, who did not consider themselves bound by the same obligations of honour and good feeling towards Gentiles as towards one another. (Compare what Launce says in *Two Gentlemen of Verona*: "Go with me to the alehouse, if not thou art an Hebrew, a Jew .... because thou hast not so much charity in thee as to go to the ale with a Christian"—with *The Merchant of Venice*, i. 3. 32, and ii. 5. 14.)

2. A very similar opinion arose in matters of religion.

[1] Mr. F. S. Boas' *Shakespeare and his Predecessors*, p. 226, in a most interest-ing study of Shylock, speaks of the speech in iii. 1. 44 as a 'majestic vindication of Judaism'. Should not this be 'of human nature'?

[2] Compare the stories told of the retirement of Tiberius, Frederick the Great, and our own William III.

[3] This belief appears as early as Juvenal, cf. *Sat.* xiv. 103, 104.

In days when the story of the New Testament was chiefly known to people through miracle plays, the fact that St. Paul and St. John, and the founder of Christianity himself, had been Jews, became forgotten or overlooked. Even to those who could and did read their Bibles, the language of the Fourth Gospel, in which 'the Jews' are constantly mentioned in opposition to Christ (see St. John v. 15; vi. 41, etc.) might easily be misunderstood. Continual dwelling on the story of the crucifixion, without reference to the rest of Jewish history, led to a belief that the Jews were an exceptionally unfeeling and cruel race,[1] and their supposed hardness of heart passed into a proverb. (Compare Launce again in *Two Gentlemen of Verona*, act ii. sc. 3, l. 12: "A Jew would have wept to have seen our parting"; and *Richard II.*, act ii. 1. 55, "Stubborn Jewry".) So that Antonio looks upon a piece of seeming kindness on Shylock's part as a sign that he may yet 'turn Christian' [   ]. Conversely, the Jewish refusal of Christianity was regarded not as intellectual negation, but as a piece of the stiff-necked perversity with which their own prophets had charged them. It must also be remembered that religious intolerance was, in "the ages of conflict", almost universal, and was displayed by the Jews themselves on a great scale during that short period of their history when they had the power of the sword over aliens in race and religion.[2] Some of the beliefs and rites of mediæval Christianity appeared to Jews to be idolatrous and blasphemous, and towards them it was lawful and right in their eyes to feel a 'lodged hate' and 'a loathing'. (See page 411 of *Jewish Life in the Middle Ages*, by I. Abrahams; Macmillan, 1896.)

3. The widespread belief that Jews were miserly and squalid

---

[1] Is it not possible to see traces of this in the description of Shylock's conduct at the trial? Compare "I stand here for law" with "The Jews answered him, We have a law, and by our law he ought to die" (St. John xix. 7); and again, "My deeds upon my head" with "His blood be on us and on our children" (St. Matthew xxvii. 25); and again, "Would any of the stock of *Barrabas* had been her husband, rather than a Christian!"

[2] In this respect Shylock's spirit is far more truly representative than the 'undenominationalism' of Lessing's *Nathan the Wise*.

Religious Feeling.

in their mode of life arose, no doubt, mainly from the fact
Alleged miserli- that for many centuries it was as much as
ness of Jews. their lives were worth to give signs of super-
fluous wealth.

But this unlovely hardness of life was only assumed by
compulsion. In reality, Jews have always been fond of a rich
and even luxurious style of living. (See *Jewish Life in the
Middle Ages*, chapters viii. and xvi.)

4. We cannot understand this ground of hatred against
Shylock without remembering that both Jews and Christians
Odium against were forbidden by their ecclesiastical law to take
usurers. interest on money from those of their own faith.
But Jews might take it from 'the stranger' (Deut. xxiii. 20),
and so it came about that when commerce increased and
loans began to be an essential part of its machinery, Jews
naturally assumed the position of money-lenders. This consequence was hastened by the very persecutions to which they
were subject. The cruel laws which in many places forbade
their plying any trade or profession recognized among Christians (see chaps. xi. and xii. of Abrahams' *Jewish Life in the
Middle Ages*) drove them to usury. The necessity for having
their property in such a shape that it could be easily 'lifted'
in case of expulsion or attack, forced them to accumulate
wealth in the form of gold and precious stones. Practice
quickly made them experts at the financier's trade, and from
their very position as aliens they were able to make that distinction between monetary and amicable relations without
which extended commerce, as we know it now, is impossible.
But the necessity for the trade did not make it popular, and
the laws against usurers, by increasing the lender's risk, kept
up the rate of interest, and aggravated the evil.

Shylock was thus one of a body who in religion and in
society kept themselves aloof in repulsive isolation, who
not only declined but abhorred the religious beliefs of their
neighbours, and who, while taught by persecution not to show
signs of wealth, were at the same time accumulating precious
metals, and obtaining a great hold over individual Christians
by their system of loans.

(*e*) In all this we see abundant explanation of such a feeling as is expressed in its most extravagant form in Marlowe's *Jew of Malta*. The humanity with which Shakespeare draws the portraiture of Shylock is therefore all the more striking. The Jew's hatred for Antonio is not represented as mere 'motiveless malignity', but as the result of injured patriotism, of commercial jealousy [   ], and of resentment aroused by repeated personal insults.

Humanity of Shakespeare's portrait.

He speaks with tenderness of a relic of his dead wife. It is not hinted that he used any further unkindness towards his daughter and his servant than to make their life extremely bleak and dull; to Jessica his tone is not harsh, and he trusts her—though with some misgivings—with all his keys. His fury over her robbery and desertion of him for the sake of a Christian lover is very comprehensible, and the frightful savagery with which it is expressed cannot fairly be taken literally, any more than Bassanio's willingness to offer Portia in sacrifice to save Antonio. Shylock's last reference to Jessica shows fatherly feeling [   ], and in Launcelot he recognizes kindness with appreciation [   ].

His great appeal to human nature [   ] is irresistible, though he fails to see its application to his own religious and racial exclusiveness.

(*f*) In summary, Shylock is a miser, but a miser possessing great strength of resolution and high powers of intellect. His main fault is not a want of feeling, but a misapplication of it. So far is he from being of an insensible, flinty character, that he rather appears excessively passionate and irritable. His cruelty is not that of a cold heart, but the more terrible cruelty of perverted and outraged sensitiveness. It comes nearer the rage of Othello than the malice of Iago. And even at his worst, when every other feeling has been absorbed in the one longing to feel his knife in his enemy's heart, even then the concentration of his purpose, the clear force of his understanding, make him a figure terrible indeed, but not despicable. There wanted but another stroke to raise him to the dignity of possessing

Summary of his character.

"The unconquerable will
And study of revenge, immortal hate,
And courage never to submit or yield,
And what is else not to be overcome".

(*g*) But his spirit bends at last, and the tale ends without a tragedy. To think of his fate as hopelessly miserable is to

His fate.

force modern notions into our reading. We must remember that to Shakespeare's audiences, conversion, even though compulsory, would mean the possibility of salvation for Shylock. Since adherence to Judaism was thought to rest not on spiritual conviction but on obstinate temper, Shylock's becoming a Christian would be regarded as a recovery from sullenness. The remission of half his goods would appear generous. The absorption of so formidable an alien into the body of the community, the marriage of his daughter to a Venetian, and the ultimate diffusion of his wealth among those willing to make a cheerful use of it, would—in those days—seem the happiest solution possible of the difficulties and dangers raised by his existence.

After a study of Shylock and Jessica, it is interesting to go back to *Ivanhoe*, and to renew one's recollections of Isaac of York and Rebecca. In what points is the novelist's portraiture weaker than the poet's?

2. PORTIA, at the opening of the story, appears without father or mother, or indeed any relative nearer than her cousin [   ], the famous jurisconsult of Padua, Doctor Bellario. Of her mother[1] we hear not a word; it seems she must have died in Portia's infancy. Her father, a wealthy

The childhood of Portia.

Italian noble, Lord of Belmont, had educated his only child with the utmost care, to speak Latin and French as well as Italian [   ], to understand law, and to manage the affairs of a great property. He lived long enough (i. 2. 97) to see her of a marriageable age, and to notice the passionate admiration roused in men of every kind by her high spirit, brilliant wit, and 'beauty

[1] Many of Shakespeare's heroines are motherless:—Isabella, Beatrice, Rosalind, Imogen, Miranda, Cordelia, Viola, Helena, Ophelia. He was interested, perhaps, rather in the relation of mother to *son*, and of father to *daughter*. Or he felt that—had their mothers been there—his maidens could never have fallen into so many perils and troubles.

like the sun', placed as these qualities were, in circumstances hardly less romantic and splendid than those of a princess of fairyland.   But, before a marriage could be arranged, he was seized with mortal sickness.   On his deathbed [   ] he willed that his daughter's hand should—under restriction severe enough to keep away mere adventurers—be won by a 'lottery'.   This 'lottery', in so far as it was matter of chance, would be—so it was thought in those days—under the ruling of Providence, and so far as it was matter of choice, would be such as to test the insight and sincerity of her lovers.

Thus was Portia, hardly yet out of her girlhood, left heiress of Belmont.   The fame of her person and character, her wealth, and the hazard by which she was to be won, drew suitors from many lands.   She watched them come with amusement, and with keenest penetration, for *Her loyalty to* she knew the points of a man.   But she was *her father's will.* loyal to her father's will, and to the oath (iii. 2. 11) which she had taken to fulfil it.   Her loyalty was proof even against her own feeling that she had already seen (i. 2. 100), in a young Venetian, a scholar and a soldier, of gentle blood but no estate, the man to whom she could give the whole of herself.

This decisive sense of honour was blended in Portia with a trained intelligence and a sense of humour.   It is this union of qualities which marks her action *Clearness in* throughout.   It enables her to see quite straight *thought and in* at moments of crisis, as when Antonio's letter *action.* comes on the eve of her marriage.   By virtue of it she discerns in an instant a *cul-de-sac* from a path, and loses no time by trying impracticable ways.   Her wit is equal to a thousand shifts, but her practised reason and her sound feeling show her the only right one.   The end once in view, she adjusts the means to it, and sets all in motion with a quickness and a swing and a lightness of touch that stamp her an artist in action.   Her alacrity is beforehand with danger, and she beats difficulty by power of combination. To her husband she gives herself with a generous complete- ness which, in one so clear-sighted, makes her words after Bassanio's choice the most moving thing of the kind in

xxvi THE MERCHANT OF VENICE.

literature. Her solution of the problem of the bond, by a bold reduction to the absurd, is of a piece with that perfect *clearness* of character which appears in Portia sometimes as wit and grace, sometimes as courage, sometimes as penetrating insight.

This extreme *directness* in thought and action gives to Portia an almost formidable air, not diminished by the trained skill with which she approaches the discussion of an abstract principle. In these respects she is unlike many others of Shakespeare's women. It needs all her wisdom to keep her wit within bounds, and she is sometimes too unmerciful to affectation (whether in a Prince of Arragon or in one of her own pages) to be perfectly courteous. But the warmth and openness of her heart, and an extreme generosity of feeling, kindle her amazing cleverness into tact, and make her great gifts available for the ordinary offices of life. Again and again she relieves embarrassment and meets a difficult moment with a grace so perfect as to show, besides dexterity, true goodness of nature (*e.g.* in her words to the Prince of Morocco when he makes apology for his complexion; or to Bassanio when, by a stinging pun, she draws attention from her own generosity in despatching him at once to the help of Antonio). Thus, although she could preach eloquently (iv. 1. 178, ff.), and argue most forcibly, she knows that sermons and arguments are comparatively futile (i. 2. 14). Though from many indications we see she was sincerely religious, she would not be content with *only* praying when she could work as well (compare v. 1. 31, with iii. 4. 30 to the end of the scene). And her delightful sense of humour saves her from any touch of self-conceit. Her spirit of comradeship and friendliness keeps her always human and kindly.

No analysis can explain the charm and power of a character like Portia's. We can perhaps best realize our feeling about her by the assurance we have that she would do nobly always, but that the full greatness of her qualities could only be shown in some crisis needing prompt and courageous

Portia is formidable;

but her friendliness saves her from pedantry.

Confidence roused by her high and noble spirit.

action. She had, indeed, along with all womanly virtues, a larger share than most women have of some qualities commonly considered masculine, which ought perhaps to be regarded as the common property of women and men :—the power to see all round a point of abstract theory, and the will to take and keep a direct line in practice. We feel certain that were Bassanio called away to the wars, and Belmont besieged by his enemy, Portia could with undismayed cheerfulness hold his house for him, command his men, keep them in heart with jests more humorous than Launcelot's, see that her children were in due order and attentive to their studies, and yet, all the while, have time to discomfit her domestic chaplain in quiet hours of chess and theology.

3. BASSANIO.—Bassanio's character is to be judged less from what he himself says or does than from the reflected picture which we get of him in the words and actions of other people. The two main points we know about him are that he is Antonio's chosen friend and Portia's chosen lover. Antonio—who knew all Venice—only loves the world for Bassanio's sake (ii. 8. 50), and for him Portia, courted by all nations and languages, would be trebled twenty times herself (iii. 2. 154). Nerissa lets us know that he is a scholar and a soldier, and that "he, of all the men that ever my foolish eyes looked upon, was the best deserving a fair lady". Gratiano 'must' travel with him, even at the cost of a more subdued behaviour. And Launcelot Gobbo, who was too lively a lad not to be an excellent judge of a man when he saw one, thinks his fortune is made when he gets into his service, poor though Bassanio was. When he appears in company, other folks pay him a kind of deference which is all the more striking that it seems unconscious, and has no possible motive but to express natural feel- His force of ing. Thus even by his familiar friends he is character. addressed as 'My Lord Bassanio', 'Signior Bassanio'. He becomes, without effort, the centre of any group in which he finds himself. The secret of his power is also the explanation of the comparatively small show which his actual words

and deeds make in a representation of the play—for of all qualities his are the least imitable by an actor. These qualities are simplicity, directness, and courage, combined with a perfect ease and kindliness of bearing and manner. Heavily in debt, he takes neither of the two easy alternatives for the poor man,—an impracticable stiffness, or a conscious humility, but borrows from his rich friend and wooes his wealthy mistress with such a natural and manly frankness as endears him further to them both. The enigma of the three caskets he solves because he 'rightly loves', and will hazard all to win. He has the gift, by nature and breeding, of doing and saying the right thing at the right time, the tact that is founded upon good sense and a kind heart.

Masterfulness. There is a fund of quiet masterfulness in his manner of giving orders: "You may do so; but let it be so hasted that supper be ready at the farthest by five of the clock. See these letters delivered; put the liveries to making, and desire Gratiano to come anon to my lodging" (ii. 2. 104). With what fine discretion he guides his words in checking the excitable Gratiano! How plainly his firmer will and clearer sense come out in contrast with that volatile but otherwise delightful character! The effect of the splendid simplicity of his qualities is heightened by the external magnificence of the rivals to whom he is preferred. Some have questioned Portia's insight, and maintained that

His truth and strength of nature give him authority. she 'threw herself away' on Bassanio. But indeed she, like the rest of the world, might have said to him much what Kent said to Lear, "You have that in your countenance which I would fain call master". "What's that?" "Authority." It is just this 'authority', or unconscious control, which, in a man, is the supreme quality. Oliver Wendell Holmes says, in speaking of a similar choice: "It takes a very *true* man to be a fitting companion for a woman of genius, but not a very great one. I am not sure that she will not embroider her ideal better on a plain ground than on one with a brilliant pattern already worked in its texture. But as the very essence of genius is truthfulness, contact with realities (which are always ideas behind shows of form or language), nothing is so contemptible as falsehood and pretence in its eyes. Now, *Portia's choice of Bassanio.* it is not easy to find a perfectly true woman, and it is very hard to find a perfectly true man. And a woman of genius, who has the sagacity to choose such a one as her companion, shows more of the divine gift in so doing than in her finest talk or her most brilliant work of letters or of art" (from chapter xii. of *The Professor at the Breakfast-table*).

4. ANTONIO was one of the chief men of that great Mediterranean city, 'whose merchants were princes, whose traffickers were the honourable of the earth'. *The spirit of Antonio's trading.* Now and again in the course of the play, an odd term or phrase brings back the very look and colour of that old Venetian trading: 'argosies' that 'richly come to harbour suddenly', 'pirates' and 'land-thieves', 'many a purchased slave', 'silks' and 'spices', a 'turquoise' and a 'diamond' that 'cost two thousand ducats', 'a beauteous scarf veiling an Indian beauty', 'parrots' of 'commendable discourse', and 'a wilderness of monkeys'. This last has a touch as of Sinbad himself in it, and, throughout, the commerce is not confined or sedentary; there is a whole volume of 'voyages' in the very names of the places from which Antonio's tall ships carry their rich lading—

> "From Tripolis, from Mexico, and England,
> From Lisbon, Barbary, and India".

The brisk movement of the piece appears in the medley of nations that find their way to Belmont—Neapolitan, Frenchman, Saxon, Spaniard, Englishman, and Moor. It has been objected to Bassanio that he makes love in the spirit of a trader, but it would be less misleading to say that Antonio trades in the spirit of a lover, like Jason and his Argonauts.

Magnanimity, indeed, is the inmost quality of the 'royal' merchant. He lives to do great kindnesses greatly,

> "the kindest man,
> The best condition'd and unwearied spirit
> In doing courtesies, and one in whom
> The ancient Roman honour more appears
> Than any that draws breath in Italy" [   ].

He associates by preference, not with merchants, but with a soldier and a scholar like Bassanio, and his friends Lorenzo and Gratiano. He is well known at court. The Duke and 'the magnificoes of greatest port' [   ] are interested in his welfare. Consistently with this, he seems not to be greatly concerned with his merchandise except as the material of his bounty; he spends large sums in relieving poor debtors from difficulty (iii. 3. 23); and he plainly says no more than the truth in telling Bassanio that to question the heartiness of his affection would hurt him more than to waste the whole of his fortune [   ].

His magnanimity.

His spirit is serious and grave, subject to fits of melancholy, full of sensibility and tenderness. He is content to enjoy life through his friend (ii. 8. 50). He 'embraces' heaviness, and tears come readily to his eyes. So full of anxious kindness is his manner that his enemy can describe him as 'fawning' [   ]. It is characteristic of him that he is sincerely resigned at the near prospect of dying; constitutional diffidence, perhaps physical weakness, make him feel that he is 'a tainted wether of the flock, meetest for death', one of 'the weakest kind of fruit' [   ]. He rather discourages the attempts of his friends to save him (iii. 3. 19; iv. 1. 77), and is satisfied to think that Bassanio will live still and write his epitaph. It is in keeping with his quiet temperament that he should put aside, almost angrily, the notion of his being in love (i. 1. 46). He is a bachelor 'predestinate', and when we lose sight of him at Belmont it is with a feeling that his main interest for the future will be the duties of a godfather.

His sensibility and seriousness.

It shocks us to find Antonio treating Shylock with gross personal discourtesy. Nothing indeed could have expressed so vividly the feeling of the time towards a Jewish usurer, as insult and violence from the stately and amiable Antonio.

The historical explanation of this feeling is suggested elsewhere.[1]

5. THE MINOR CHARACTERS.—1. Of the other persons of the play, *Jessica* and *Lorenzo* influence the story most. Jessica we are to think of as scarcely more than a child. Her mother had apparently been dead *Jessica.* some years. Bright, winsome, and vivacious, Jessica feels she is not her father's daughter [   ], at least in 'manners'. Fond of movement and company, she saw no one at home but such as Tubal and Chus, grim men of business with whom her father talked of his design on the life of Antonio [   ]. Such a scheme must have terrified her as much as his dislike of masques and fifes repelled her [   ]. Out of Shylock's house she passes as flightily and almost as unfeelingly as a fledged bird that leaves the nest [   ]. It is not 'her way' to scruple or reflect. She takes jewels and ducats as lightly as she goes herself; she had never seen any pleasant use made of either, and, if she thought at all, she may have thought her father would not miss what he never wore nor spent. She talks very much too freely to Launcelot Gobbo. Her natural recklessness of temper appears from the style in which she makes the money fly at Genoa. (What kind of sitting was it, at which she spent fourscore ducats?) It is exquisitely characteristic in her to buy a monkey for a pet; no doubt Lorenzo took care it was left behind in Genoa. On her first arrival at Belmont she becomes amusingly 'proper' and quiet. Portia was a revelation to her, and in her presence, as at the sound of sweet music, Jessica's 'spirits are attentive' and she cannot be 'merry'. Her words of enthusiastic praise to Lorenzo [   ] are the least inadequate that have ever been uttered about 'my Lord Bassanio's wife'. They show that she really is susceptible to strong feeling when she meets what is superlatively good. Possibly Lorenzo's confidence that she is 'true' as well as 'fair and wise' [   ] may, after all, be realized, if circumstances favour her.

[1] See page xx.

Her husband, though possessed of deeper feelings and of much more power of thought than Jessica, yet looks on life Lorenzo. from much the same point of view. He is intensely alive to delight, whether in natural beauty or in music. But his taste is so sound that, even by moonlight, his is a 'waking bliss', full of 'sober certainty' as well as of the richest poetic rapture. Twice, in our short acquaintance with him, his sense of humour saves sentiment from extravagance or unreality (iii. 5. 58; v. 1. 15). He is, as he admits, 'unthrift', and we may conjecture with much probability that his intimacy with Jessica began in visits to Shylock for severely business purposes. But the future of the pair in matters of finance is assured by the fact that they are to have a kind and careful trustee in the person of the Merchant of Venice himself.

2. Of the rest, *Gratiano* is talkative and gregarious to a fault, but he is excellent company and says some admirable Gratiano.. things. There is, as Hazlitt says, a whole volume of philosophy in his sermon against silence [   ], and his words in ii. 6. 8 ff show imagination. A man of his qualities may be tiresome in a small party, but is invaluable in a company of a dozen or more, where his loquacity can be 'absorbed'. His wife will be the best possible match for him. Their conversation may indeed 'overlap' somewhat, for Nerissa has her own reflections on life and can 'pronounce them well' and 'in good sentences'. But they are both too good-natured for the house ever to be seriously 'unquiet' (iv. 1. 288).

3. On the Princes of Morocco and Arragon, see notes to the scenes in which they appear.

4. *Launcelot Gobbo* is the 'wag' of the piece. His humour consists chiefly in a misuse of long words and in the liveliest Launcelot. animal spirits. There is less wit in what he says than is the case with any other of the prominent 'clowns' or 'fools' in Shakespeare. He is ready for any mischief, 'a huge feeder', and so averse to 'working between meals' that Shylock has to employ three similes in two lines ('snail', 'drone', and 'wild cat') to express the

(M 330)

extent of his laziness.   But even Shylock recognises that he is 'kind enough', and Bassanio takes to him immediately [   ].

5. The characters of *Salarino* and *Salanio* are not further defined than that they are Venetian gentleman, friends of Antonio and Bassanio, and full of the ordinary feeling of the time against Jewish usurers.

5. DATE OF THE COMPOSITION OF THE PLAY.

The Merchant of Venice was first printed in 1600, when it appeared by itself in two quarto editions, one, called the First Quarto, published by James Roberts, the other, the Second Quarto, by Thomas Heyes.   It had been in existence at least two years before, for on the 22nd of July, 1598, it was entered in the Stationers' Register by James Roberts under the name of 'a booke of the Marchaunt of Venyce or otherwise called the Jewe of Venice'.   And, in the same year, 1598, appeared the *Palladis Tamia* or *Wit's Treasury*, by Francis Meres, who names the following comedies of Shakespeare: 'his Gentlemen of Verona, his Errors, his Love labors lost, his Love labours wonne, his Midsummers night dreame, and his Merchant of Venice'.

So far as 'external evidence' goes, therefore,[1] we can be certain that the play was not written later than the end of 1597.

All attempts to fix the date more precisely than this rest upon unsatisfactory evidence.   For instance, much use has been made of the fact that in the account-book of Philip Henslowe, proprietor of the theatre where Shakespeare's fellow-actors were playing between 1594 and 1596, we find under the date 25th August, 1594, a reference to the performance of a new play, the *Venesyon Comodey*.   But there is no sort of proof that this is Shakespeare's play.   Again,

---

[1] For the different kinds of evidence obtainable in settling the date of one of Shakespeare's plays, see the admirable summary in chapter iv. of Professor Dowden's *Shakspere Primer*.

some have seen a close resemblance between Shylock's argument in the trial scene as to the treatment of slaves and the argument of a Jew contained in Silvayn's *Orator*, which was published in 1596. But the differences are at least as striking as the resemblance.

In manner, *The Merchant of Venice* is near akin to *Twelfth Night*, *As You Like It*, and *Much Ado About Nothing*. With these plays of Shakespeare's 'middle' period, it has much more in common than with the earlier comedies mentioned along with it by Francis Meres. This is particularly conspicuous in the free employment of prose, even in scenes of serious interest, and in the easy and varied rhythm of the verse. We ought not perhaps to make much of the fact that it is the *last* in Meres' list. But on general grounds it seems safe to believe that *The Merchant of Venice* was written only a short time before the *Palladis Tamia* appeared, and that 1597 is therefore its probable date.

THE MERCHANT

OF

VENICE

DRAMATIS PERSONÆ

The DUKE OF VENICE.
The PRINCE OF MOROCCO, } suitors to Portia.
The PRINCE OF ARRAGON, }
ANTONIO, a Merchant of Venice.
BASSANIO, his friend, suitor likewise to Portia.
SALANIO, }
SALARINO, } friends to Antonio and Bassanio.
GRATIANO, }
LORENZO, in love with Jessica.
SHYLOCK, a rich Jew.
TUBAL, a Jew, his friend.
LAUNCELOT GOBBO, the clown, servant to Shylock.
OLD GOBBO, father to Launcelot.
LEONARDO, servant to Bassanio.
BALTHASAR, } servants to Portia.
STEPHANO, }

PORTIA, a rich heiress.
NERISSA, her waiting-maid.
JESSICA, daughter to Shylock.

Magnificoes of Venice, Officers of the Court of Justice, Gaoler, Servants to Portia, and other Attendants

SCENE: *Partly at Venice, and partly at Belmont, the seat of Portia on the Continent.*

THE
MERCHANT OF VENICE.

ACT I.

SCENE I. *Venice. A street.*

Enter ANTONIO, SALARINO, *and* SALANIO.

Ant. In sooth, I know not why I am so sad:
It wearies me; you say it wearies you;
But how I caught it, found it, or came by it,
What stuff 't is made of, whereof it is born,
I am to learn;
And such a want-wit sadness makes of me,
That I have much ado to know myself.
    Salar. Your mind is tossing on the ocean;
There, where your argosies with portly sail,
Like signiors and rich burghers on the flood,   10
Or, as it were, the pageants of the sea,
Do overpeer the petty traffickers,
That curtsy to them, do them reverence,
As they fly by them with their woven wings.
    Salan. Believe me, sir, had I such venture **forth,**
The better part of my affections would
Be with my hopes abroad.   I should be still
Plucking the grass, to know where sits the wind,
Peering in maps for ports and piers and roads;
And every object that might make me fear   20

1

Misfortune to my ventures, out of doubt
Would make me sad.

Salar. My wind cooling my broth
Would blow me to an ague, when I thought
What harm a wind too great at sea might do.
I should not see the sandy hour-glass run,
But I should think of shallows and of flats,
And see my wealthy Andrew dock'd in sand,
Vailing her high-top lower than her ribs
To kiss her burial. Should I go to church
And see the holy edifice of stone, 30
And not bethink me straight of dangerous rocks,
Which touching but my gentle vessel's side,
Would scatter all her spices on the stream,
Enrobe the roaring waters with my silks,
And, in a word, but even now worth this,
And now worth nothing? Shall I have the thought
To think on this, and shall I lack the thought
That such a thing bechanced would make me sad?
But tell not me; I know, Antonio
Is sad to think upon his merchandise. 40

Ant. Believe me, no: I thank my fortune for it,
My ventures are not in one bottom trusted,
Nor to one place; nor is my whole estate
Upon the fortune of this present year:
Therefore my merchandise makes me not sad.

Salar. Why, then you are in love.

Ant. Fie, fie!

Salar. Not in love neither? Then let us say you are sad,
Because you are not merry: and 't were as easy
For you to laugh and leap and say you are merry,
Because you are not sad. Now, by two-headed Janus, 50
Nature hath framed strange fellows in her time:
Some that will evermore peep through their eyes
And laugh like parrots at a bag-piper,

And other of such vinegar aspect
That they 'll not show their teeth in way of smile,
Though Nestor swear the jest be laughable.

Enter BASSANIO, LORENZO, *and* GRATIANO.

Salan. Here comes Bassanio, your most noble kinsman,
Gratiano and Lorenzo.   Fare ye well:
We leave you now with better company.

Salar. I would have stay'd till I had made you merry, 60
If worthier friends had not prevented me.

Ant. Your worth is very dear in my regard.
I take it, your own business calls on you
And you embrace the occasion to depart.

Salar. Good morrow, my good lords.

Bass. Good signiors both, when shall we laugh? say, when?
You grow exceeding strange: must it be so?

Salar. We 'll make our leisures to attend on yours.

[*Exeunt Salarino and Salanio.*

Lor. My Lord Bassanio, since you have found Antonio,
We two will leave you: but at dinner-time,   70
I pray you, have in mind where we must meet.

Bass. I will not fail you.

Gra. You look not well, Signior Antonio;
You have too much respect upon the world:
They lose it that do buy it with much care:
Believe me, you are marvellously changed.

Ant. I hold the world but as the world, Gratiano;
A stage where every man must play a part,
And mine a sad one.

Gra.   Let me play the fool:
With mirth and laughter let old wrinkles come,   80
And let my liver rather heat with wine
Than my heart cool with mortifying groans.
Why should a man, whose blood is warm within,
Sit like his grandsire cut in alabaster?

Sleep when he wakes and creep into the jaundice
By being peevish?   I tell thee what, Antonio—
I love thee, and it is my love that speaks—
There are a sort of men whose visages
Do cream and mantle like a standing pond,
And do a wilful stillness entertain,   90
With purpose to be dress'd in an opinion
Of wisdom, gravity, profound conceit,
As who should say ' I am Sir Oracle,
And when I ope my lips let no dog bark!'
O my Antonio, I do know of these
That therefore only are reputed wise
For saying nothing, when, I am very sure,
If they should speak, would almost damn those ears
Which, hearing them, would call their brothers fools.
I 'll tell thee more of this another time: 100
But fish not, with this melancholy bait,
For this fool gudgeon, this opinion.
Come, good Lorenzo.   Fare ye well awhile:
I 'll end my exhortation after dinner.

   Lor. Well, we will leave you then till dinner-time:
I must be one of these same dumb wise men,
For Gratiano never lets me speak.

   Gra. Well, keep me company but two years moe,
Thou shalt not know the sound of thine own tongue.

   Ant. Farewell: I 'll grow a talker for this gear.   110

   Gra. Thanks, i' faith, for silence is only commendable
In a neat's tongue dried.   [*Exeunt Gratiano and Lorenzo.*

   Ant. Is that any thing now?

   Bass. Gratiano speaks an infinite deal of nothing, more
than any man in all Venice. His reasons are as two grains
of wheat hid in two bushels of chaff: you shall seek all day
ere you find them, and when you have them, they are not
worth the search.

   Ant. Well, tell me now what lady is the same

To whom you swore a secret pilgrimage,   120
That you to-day promised to tell me of?
  Bass. 'T is not unknown to you, Antonio,
How much I have disabled mine estate,
By something showing a more swelling port
Than my faint means would grant continuance:
Nor do I now make moan to be abridged
From such a noble rate; but my chief care
Is to come fairly off from the great debts
Wherein my time something too prodigal
Hath left me gaged.   To you, Antonio,   130
I owe the most, in money and in love,
And from your love I have a warranty
To unburden all my plots and purposes
How to get clear of all the debts I owe.
  Ant. I pray you, good Bassanio, let me know it;
And if it stand, as you yourself still do,
Within the eye of honour, be assured,
My purse, my person, my extremest means,
Lie all unlock'd to your occasions.
  Bass. In my school-days, when I had lost one shaft,   140
I shot his fellow of the self-same flight
The self-same way with more advised watch,
To find the other forth, and by adventuring both
I oft found both: I urge this childhood proof,
Because what follows is pure innocence.
I owe you much, and, like a wilful youth,
That which I owe is lost; but if you please
To shoot another arrow that self way
Which you did shoot the first, I do not doubt,
As I will watch the aim, or to find both   150
Or bring your latter hazard back again
And thankfully rest debtor for the first.
  Ant. You know me well, and herein spend but time
To wind about my love with circumstance;

B 2

And out of doubt you do me now more wrong
In making question of my uttermost
Than if you had made waste of all I have:
Then do but say to me what I should do
That in your knowledge may by me be done,
And I am prest unto it: therefore, speak.   160

   Bass. In Belmont is a lady richly left;
And she is fair and, fairer than that word,
Of wondrous virtues: sometimes from her eyes
I did receive fair speechless messages:
Her name is Portia, nothing undervalued
To Cato's daughter, Brutus' Portia:
Nor is the wide world ignorant of her worth,
For the four winds blow in from every coast
Renowned suitors, and her sunny locks
Hang on her temples like a golden fleece;   170
Which makes her seat of Belmont Colchos' strand,
And many Jasons come in quest of her.
O my Antonio, had I but the means
To hold a rival place with one of them,
I have a mind presages me such thrift,
That I should questionless be fortunate!

   Ant. Thou know'st that all my fortunes are at sea;
Neither have I money nor commodity
To raise a present sum: therefore go forth;
Try what my credit can in Venice do: 180
That shall be rack'd, even to the uttermost,
To furnish thee to Belmont, to fair Portia.
Go, presently inquire, and so will I,
Where money is, and I no question make
To have it of my trust or for my sake.   [*Exeunt.*

SCENE II. *Belmont. A room in* PORTIA'S *house.*

Enter PORTIA *and* NERISSA.

Por. By my troth, Nerissa, my little body is aweary of this great world.

Ner. You would be, sweet madam, if your miseries were in the same abundance as your good fortunes are: and yet, for aught I see, they are as sick that surfeit with too much as they that starve with nothing. It is no mean happiness therefore, to be seated in the mean: superfluity comes sooner by white hairs, but competency lives longer.

Por. Good sentences and well pronounced.

Ner. They would be better, if well followed.   10

Por. If to do were as easy as to know what were good to do, chapels had been churches and poor men's cottages princes' palaces. It is a good divine that follows his own instructions: I can easier teach twenty what were good to be done, than be one of the twenty to follow mine own teaching. The brain may devise laws for the blood, but a hot temper leaps o'er a cold decree: such a hare is madness the youth, to skip o'er the meshes of good counsel the cripple. But this reasoning is not in the fashion to choose me a husband. O me, the word ' choose '! I may neither choose whom I would nor refuse whom I dislike; so is the will of a living daughter curbed by the will of a dead father. Is it not hard, Nerissa, that I cannot choose one nor refuse none?   24

Ner. Your father was ever virtuous; and holy men at their death have good inspirations: therefore the lottery, that he hath devised in these three chests of gold, silver and lead, whereof who chooses his meaning chooses you, will, no doubt, never be chosen by any rightly but one who shall rightly love. But what warmth is there in your affection towards any of these princely suitors that are already come?

Por. I pray thee, over-name them; and as thou namest them, I will describe them; and, according to my description, level at my affection.   34

Ner. First, there is the Neapolitan prince.

Por. Ay, that 's a colt indeed, for he doth nothing but talk of his horse; and he makes it a great appropriation to his own good parts, that he can shoe him himself.

Ner. Then there is the County Palatine.

Por. He doth nothing but frown, as who should say ' If you will not have me, choose ': he hears merry tales and smiles not: I fear he will prove the weeping philosopher when he grows old, being so full of unmannerly sadness in his youth. I had rather be married to a death's-head with a bone in his mouth than to either of these. God defend me from these two!   46

Ner. How say you by the French lord, Monsieur Le Bon?

Por. God made him, and therefore let him pass for a man. In truth, I know it is a sin to be a mocker: but, he! why, he hath a horse better than the Neapolitan's, a better bad habit of frowning than the Count Palatine; he is every man in no man; if a throstle sing, he falls straight a capering: he will fence with his own shadow: if I should marry him, I should marry twenty husbands. If he would despise me, I would forgive him, for if he love me to madness, I shall never requite him.   56

Ner. What say you, then, to Falconbridge, the young baron of England?

Por. You know I say nothing to him, for he understands not me, nor I him: he hath neither Latin, French, nor Italian, and you will come into the court and swear that I have a poor pennyworth in the English. He is a proper man's picture, but, alas, who can converse with a dumb-show? How oddly he is suited! I think he bought his doublet in Italy, his round hose in France, his bonnet in Germany and his behaviour every where.   66

Ner. What think you of the Scottish lord, his neighbour?

Por. That he hath a neighbourly charity in him, for he borrowed a box of the ear of the Englishman and swore he would pay him again when he was able: I think the Frenchman became his surety and sealed under for another.

Ner. How like you the young German, the Duke of Saxony's nephew? 73

Por. Very vilely in the morning, when he is sober, and most vilely in the afternoon, when he is drunk: when he is best, he is a little worse than a man, and when he is worst, he is little better than a beast: an the worst fall that ever fell, I hope I shall make shift to go without him.

Ner. If he should offer to choose, and choose the right casket, you should refuse to perform your father's will, if you should refuse to accept him. 81

Por. Therefore, for fear of the worst, I pray thee, set a deep glass of rhenish wine on the contrary casket, for if the devil be within and that temptation without, I know he will choose it. I will do any thing, Nerissa, ere I 'll be married to a sponge.

Ner. You need not fear, lady, the having any of these lords: they have acquainted me with their determinations; which is, indeed, to return to their home and to trouble you with no more suit, unless you may be won by some other sort than your father's imposition depending on the caskets.

Por. If I live to be as old as Sibylla, I will die as chaste as Diana, unless I be obtained by the manner of my father's will. I am glad this parcel of wooers are so reasonable, for there is not one among them but I dote on his very absence, and I pray God grant them a fair departure. 96

Ner. Do you not remember, lady, in your father's time, a Venetian, a scholar and a soldier, that came hither in company of the Marquis of Montferrat?

Por. Yes, yes, it was Bassanio; as I think, he was so called.

Ner. True, madam: he, of all the men that ever my foolish eyes looked upon, was the best deserving a fair lady.

Por. I remember him well, and I remember him worthy of thy praise.   105

Enter a Serving-man.

How now! what news?

Serv. The four strangers seek for you, madam, to take their leave: and there is a forerunner come from a fifth, the Prince of Morocco, who brings word the prince his master will be here to-night.   110

Por. If I could bid the fifth welcome with so good a heart as I can bid the other four farewell, I should be glad of his approach: if he have the condition of a saint and the complexion of a devil, I had rather he should shrive me than wive me.

Come, Nerissa. Sirrah, go before.
Whiles we shut the gates upon one wooer, another knocks at
the door.   [*Exeunt.*

SCENE III.   *Venice.   A public place.*

Enter BASSANIO *and* SHYLOCK.

Shy. Three thousand ducats; well.

Bass. Ay, sir, for three months.

Shy. For three months; well.

Bass. For the which, as I told you, Antonio shall be bound.

Shy. Antonio shall become bound; well.

Bass. May you stead me? will you pleasure me? shall I know your answer?

Shy. Three thousand ducats for three months and Antonio bound.

Bass. Your answer to that.   10

Shy. Antonio is a good man.

Bass. Have you heard any imputation to the contrary?

Shy. Oh, no, no, no, no: my meaning in saying he is a good man is to have you understand me that he is sufficient. Yet his means are in supposition: he hath an argosy bound to Tripolis, another to the Indies; I understand, moreover, upon the Rialto, he hath a third at Mexico, a fourth for England, and other ventures he hath, squandered abroad. But ships are but boards, sailors but men: there be land-rats and water-rats, water-thieves and land-thieves, I mean pirates, and then there is the peril of waters, winds and rocks. The man is, notwithstanding, sufficient. Three thousand ducats; I think I may take his bond.   23

Bass. Be assured you may.

Shy. I will be assured I may; and, that I may be assured, I will bethink me. May I speak with Antonio?

Bass. If it please you to dine with us.

Shy. Yes, to smell pork; to eat of the habitation which your prophet the Nazarite conjured the devil into. I will buy with you, sell with you, talk with you, walk with you, and so following, but I will not eat with you, drink with you, nor pray with you. What news on the Rialto? Who is he comes here?   33

Enter ANTONIO.

Bass. This is Signior Antonio.

Shy. [*Aside*] How like a fawning publican he looks!
I hate him for he is a Christian,
But more for that in low simplicity
He lends out money gratis and brings down
The rate of usance here with us in Venice.
If I can catch him once upon the hip,   40
I will feed fat the ancient grudge I bear him.
He hates our sacred nation, and he rails,
Even there where merchants most do congregate,
On me, my bargains and my well-won thrift,

Which he calls interest. Cursed be my tribe,
If I forgive him!

    Bass.   Shylock, do you hear?

    Shy. I am debating of my present store,
And, by the near guess of my memory,
I cannot instantly raise up the gross
Of full three thousand ducats. What of that?   50
Tubal, a wealthy Hebrew of my tribe,
Will furnish me. But soft! how many months
Do you desire? [*To Ant.*] Rest you fair, good signior;
Your worship was the last man in our mouths.

    Ant. Shylock, although I neither lend nor borrow
By taking nor by giving of excess,
Yet, to supply the ripe wants of my friend,
I 'll break a custom. Is he yet possess'd
How much ye would?

    Shy.   Ay, ay, three thousand ducats.

    Ant. And for three months.   60

    Shy. I had forgot; three months; you told me so.
Well then, your bond; and let me see; but hear you;
Methought you said you neither lend nor borrow
Upon advantage.

    Ant.   I do never use it.

    Shy. When Jacob grazed his uncle Laban's sheep—
This Jacob from our holy Abram was,
As his wise mother wrought in his behalf,
The third possessor; ay, he was the third—

    Ant. And what of him? did he take interest?

    Shy. No, not take interest. not, as you would say,   70
Directly interest: mark what Jacob did.
When Laban and himself were compromised
That all the eanlings which were streaked and pied
Should fall as Jacob's hire,
The skilful shepherd pilled me certain wands
And stuck them up before the fulsome ewes,

Who, then conceiving, did in eaning time
Fall party-coloured lambs, and those were Jacob's.
This was a way to thrive, and he was blest;
And thrift is blessing, if men steal it not.   80
  Ant. This was a venture, sir, that Jacob served for;
A thing not in his power to bring to pass,
But sway'd and fashion'd by the hand of heaven.
Was this inserted to make interest good?
Or is your gold and silver ewes and rams?
  Shy. I cannot tell; I make it breed as fast:
But note me, signior.
  Ant.   Mark you this, Bassanio,
The devil can cite Scripture for his purpose.
An evil soul producing holy witness
Is like a villain with a smiling cheek,   90
A goodly apple rotten at the heart:
O, what a goodly outside falsehood hath!
  Shy. Three thousand ducats; 't is a good round sum.
Three months from twelve; then, let me see; the rate—
  Ant. Well, Shylock, shall we be beholding to you?
  Shy. Signior Antonio, many a time and oft
In the Rialto you have rated me
About my money and my usances:
Still have I borne it with a patient shrug,
For sufferance is the badge of all our tribe.   100
You call me misbeliever, cut-throat dog,
And spit upon my Jewish gaberdine,
And all for use of that which is mine own.
Well then, it now appears you need my help:
Go to, then; you come to me, and you say
' Shylock, we would have moneys ': you say so;
You, that did void your rheum upon my beard
And foot me as you spurn a stranger cur
Over your threshold: moneys is your suit.
What should I say to you?   Should I not say   110

' Hath a dog money? is it possible
A cur can lend three thousand ducats?'   Or
Shall I bend low and in a bondman's key,
With bated breath and whispering humbleness,
Say this;
' Fair sir, you spit on me on Wednesday last;
You spurn'd me such a day; another time
You call'd me dog; and for these courtesies
I 'll lend you thus much moneys '?
   Ant. I am as like to call thee so again,   120
To spit on thee again, to spurn thee too.
If thou wilt lend this money, lend it not
As to thy friends; for when did friendship take
A breed for barren metal of his friend?
But lend it rather to thine enemy,
Who, if he break, thou mayst with better face
Exact the penalty.
   Shy.   Why, look you, how you storm!
I would be friends with you and have your love,
Forget the shames that you have stain'd me with,
Supply your present wants and take no doit   130
Of usance for my moneys, and you 'll not hear me:
This is kind I offer.
   Bass.   This were kindness.
   Shy.   This kindness will I show.
Go with me to a notary, seal me there
Your single bond; and, in a merry sport,
If you repay me not on such a day,
In such a place, such sum or sums as are
Express'd in the condition, let the forfeit
Be nominated for an equal pound
Of your fair flesh, to be cut off and taken
In what part of your body pleaseth me.   140
   Ant. Content, i' faith: I 'll seal to such a bond
And say there is much kindness in the Jew.

Bass. You shall not seal to such a bond for me:
I 'll rather dwell in my necessity.

Ant. Why, fear not, man; I will not forfeit it:
Within these two months, that 's a month before
This bond expires, I do expect return
Of thrice three times the value of this bond.

Shy. O father Abram, what these Christians are,
Whose own hard dealings teaches them suspect   150
The thoughts of others! Pray you, tell me this;
If he should break his day, what should I gain
By the exaction of the forfeiture?
A pound of man's flesh taken from a man
Is not so estimable, profitable neither,
As flesh of muttons, beefs, or goats. I say,
To buy his favour, I extend this friendship:
If he will take it, so; if not, adieu;
And, for my love, I pray you wrong me not.

Ant. Yes, Shylock, I will seal unto this bond.   160

Shy. Then meet me forthwith at the notary's;
Give him direction for this merry bond,
And I will go and purse the ducats straight,
See to my house, left in the fearful guard
Of an unthrifty knave, and presently
I will be with you.

Ant.   Hie thee, gentle Jew. [*Exit Shylock.*
The Hebrew will turn Christian: he grows kind.

Bass. I like not fair terms and a villain's mind.

Ant. Come on: in this there can be no dismay;
My ships come home a month before the day. [*Exeunt.* 170

ACT II.

Scene I. *Belmont. A room in* Portia's *house.*

Flourish of cornets. Enter the Prince of Morocco *and his train;* Portia, Nerissa, *and others attending.*

Mor. Mislike me not for my complexion,
The shadow'd livery of the burnish'd sun,
To whom I am a neighbour and near bred.
Bring me the fairest creature northward born,
Where Phœbus' fire scarce thaws the icicles,
And let us make incision for your love,
To prove whose blood is reddest, his or mine.
I tell thee, lady, this aspect of mine
Hath fear'd the valiant: by my love, I swear
The best-regarded virgins of our clime   10
Have loved it too: I would not change this hue,
Except to steal your thoughts, my gentle queen.
    Por. In terms of choice I am not solely led
By nice direction of a maiden's eyes;
Besides, the lottery of my destiny
Bars me the right of voluntary choosing:
But if my father had not scanted me
And hedged me by his wit, to yield myself
His wife who wins me by that means I told you,
Yourself, renowned prince, then stood as fair   20
As any comer I have look'd on yet
For my affection.
    Mor.   Even for that I thank you:
Therefore, I pray you, lead me to the caskets
To try my fortune. By this scimitar
That slew the Sophy and a Persian prince
That won three fields of Sultan Solyman,
I would outstare the sternest eyes that look,

Outbrave the heart most daring on the earth,
Pluck the young sucking cubs from the she-bear,
Yea, mock the lion when he roars for prey,   30
To win thee, lady.   But, alas the while!
If Hercules and Lichas play at dice
Which is the better man, the greater throw
May turn by fortune from the weaker hand:
So is Alcides beaten by his page;
And so may I, blind fortune leading me,
Miss that which one unworthier may attain,
And die with grieving.
      Por.   You must take your chance,
And either not attempt to choose at all
Or swear before you choose, if you choose wrong   40
Never to speak to lady afterward
In way of marriage: therefore be advised.
      Mor. Nor will not.   Come, bring me unto my chance
      Por. First, forward to the temple: after dinner
Your hazard shall be made.
      Mor.   Good fortune then!
To make me blest or cursed'st among men.
                                    [*Cornets, and exeunt.*

SCENE II.   *Venice.   A street.*

Enter LAUNCELOT.

Laun. Certainly my conscience will serve me to run from
this Jew my master. The fiend is at mine elbow and tempts
me saying to me 'Gobbo, Launcelot Gobbo, good Launcelot',
or 'good Gobbo', or 'good Launcelot Gobbo, use your legs,
take the start, run away '. My conscience says ' No; take
heed, honest Launcelot; take heed, honest Gobbo ', or, as
aforesaid, 'honest Launcelot Gobbo; do not run; scorn run-
ning with thy heels'. Well, the most courageous fiend bids

me pack: ' Via!' says the fiend; ' away!' says the fiend; ' for the heavens, rouse up a brave mind ', says the fiend, ' and run '. Well, my conscience, hanging about the neck of my heart, says very wisely to me ' My honest friend Launcelot, being an honest man's son', or rather an honest woman's son; for, indeed, my father did something smack, something grow to, he had a kind of taste; well, my conscience says 'Launcelot, budge not '. 'Budge', says the fiend. 'Budge not', says my conscience. ' Conscience ', say I, ' you counsel well '; 'Fiend', say I, 'you counsel well': to be ruled by my conscience, I should stay with the Jew my master, who, God bless the mark, is a kind of devil; and, to run away from the Jew, I should be ruled by the fiend, who, saving your reverence, is the devil himself. Certainly the Jew is the very devil incarnal; and, in my conscience, my conscience is but a kind of hard conscience, to offer to counsel me to stay with the Jew. The fiend gives the more friendly counsel: I will run, fiend; my heels are at your command; I will run.   26

Enter Old GOBBO, *with a basket.*

Gob. Master young man, you, I pray you, which is the way to master Jew's?

Laun. [*Aside*] O heavens, this is my true-begotten father! who, being more than sand-blind, high-gravel blind, knows me not: I will try confusions with him.

Gob. Master young gentleman, I pray you, which is the way to master Jew's?

Laun. Turn up on your right hand at the next turning, but, at the next turning of all, on your left; marry, at the very next turning, turn of no hand, but turn down indirectly to the Jew's house.   37

Gob. By God's sonties, 't will be a hard way to hit. Can you tell me whether one Launcelot, that dwells with him, dwell with him or no?

Laun. Talk you of young Master Launcelot? [*Aside*] Mark

me now; now will I raise the waters. Talk you of young
Master Launcelot?

Gob. No master, sir, but a poor man's son: his father,
though I say it, is an honest exceeding poor man and, God
be thanked, well to live.   46

Laun. Well, let his father be what a' will, we talk of young
Master Launcelot.

Gob. Your worship's friend and Launcelot, sir.

Laun. But I pray you, ergo, old man, ergo, I beseech you,
talk you of young Master Launcelot?

Gob. Of Launcelot, an 't please your mastership.   52

Laun. Ergo, Master Launcelot. Talk not of Master
Launcelot, father; for the young gentleman, according to
Fates and Destinies and such odd sayings, the Sisters Three
and such branches of learning, is indeed deceased, or, as you
would say in plain terms, gone to heaven.

Gob. Marry, God forbid! the boy was the very staff of my
age, my very prop.

Laun. Do I look like a cudgel or a hovel-post, a staff or a
prop? Do you know me, father?   61

Gob. Alack the day, I know you not, young gentleman:
but, I pray you, tell me, is my boy, God rest his soul, alive or
dead?

Laun. Do you not know me, father?

Gob. Alack, sir, I am sand-blind; I know you not.

Laun. Nay, indeed, if you had your eyes, you might fail of
the knowing me: it is a wise father that knows his own child.
Well, old man, I will tell you news of your son: give me your
blessing: truth will come to light; murder cannot be hid long;
a man's son may, but at the length truth will out.   71

Gob. Pray you, sir, stand up: I am sure you are not
Launcelot, my boy.

Laun. Pray you, let 's have no more fooling about it, but
give me your blessing: I am Launcelot, your boy that was,
your son that is, your child that shall be.

Gob. I cannot think you are my son.

Laun. I know not what I shall think of that: but I am Launcelot, the Jew's man, and I am sure Margery your wife is my mother. 80

Gob. Her name is Margery, indeed: I 'll be sworn, if thou be Launcelot, thou art mine own flesh and blood. Lord worshipped might he be! what a beard hast thou got! thou hast got more hair on thy chin than Dobbin my fill-horse has on his tail.

Laun. It should seem, then, that Dobbin's tail grows backward: I am sure he had more hair of this tail than I have of my face when I last saw him.

Gob. Lord, how art thou changed! How dost thou and thy master agree? I have brought him a present. How 'gree you now? 91

Laun. Well, well: but, for mine own part, as I have set up my rest to run away, so I will not rest till I have run some ground. My master's a very Jew: give him a present! give him a halter: I am famished in his service; you may tell every finger I have with my ribs. Father, I am glad you are come: give me your present to one Master Bassanio, who, indeed, gives rare new liveries: if I serve not him, I will run as far as God has any ground. O rare fortune! here comes the man: to him, father; for I am a Jew, if I serve the Jew any longer. 101

Enter BASSANIO, *with* LEONARDO *and other followers.*

Bass. You may do so; but let it be so hasted that supper be ready at the farthest by five of the clock. See these letters delivered; put the liveries to making, and desire Gratiano to come anon to my lodging.   [*Exit a Servant*

Laun. To him, father.

Gob. God bless your worship!

Bass. Gramercy! wouldst thou aught with me?

Gob. Here 's my son, sir, a poor boy,—

Laun. Not a poor boy, sir, but the rich Jew's man; that would, sir, as my father shall specify—   111

Gob. He hath a great infection, sir, as one would say, to serve,—

Laun. Indeed, the short and the long is, I serve the Jew, and have a desire, as my father shall specify—

Gob. His master and he, saving your worship's reverence, are scarce cater-cousins—

Laun. To be brief, the very truth is that the Jew, having done me wrong, doth cause me, as my father, being, I hope, an old man, shall frutify unto you—   120

Gob. I have here a dish of doves that I would bestow upon your worship, and my suit is—

Laun. In very brief, the suit is impertinent to myself, as your worship shall know by this honest old man; and, though I say it, though old man, yet poor man, my father.

Bass. One speak for both. What would you?

Laun. Serve you, sir.

Gob. That is the very defect of the matter, sir.

Bass. I know thee well; thou hast obtain'd thy suit: Shylock thy master spoke with me this day,   130
And hath preferr'd thee, if it be preferment
To leave a rich Jew's service, to become
The follower of so poor a gentleman.

Laun. The old proverb is very well parted between my master Shylock and you, sir: you have the grace of God, sir, and he hath enough.

Bass. Thou speak'st it well. Go, father, with thy son.
Take leave of thy old master and inquire
My lodging out. Give him a livery
More guarded than his fellows': see it done.   140

Laun. Father, in. I cannot get a service, no; I have ne'er a tongue in my head. Well, if any man in Italy have a fairer table which doth offer to swear upon a book, I shall have good fortune. Go to. here 's a simple line of life: here 's a

small trifle of wives: alas, fifteen wives is nothing! eleven
widows and nine maids is a simple coming-in for one man:
and then to 'scape drowning thrice, and to be in peril of my
life with the edge of a feather-bed; here are simple scapes.
Well, if Fortune be a woman, she 's a good wench for this
gear. Father, come; I 'll take my leave of the Jew in the
twinkling of an eye.   [*Exeunt Launcelot and Old Gobbo.*

Bass. I pray thee, good Leonardo, think on this: 152
These things being bought and orderly bestow'd,
Return in haste, for I do feast to-night
My best-esteem'd acquaintance: hie thee, go.

Leon. My best endeavours shall be done herein.

Enter GRATIANO.

Gra. Where is your master?
Leon.   Yonder, sir, he walks.   [*Exit.*
Gra. Signior Bassanio!
Bass. Gratiano!
Gra. I have a suit to you.
Bass.   You have obtain'd it.   160
Gra. You must not deny me: I must go with you to
Belmont.
Bass. Why, then you must.   But hear thee, Gratiano;
Thou art too wild, too rude and bold of voice;
Parts that become thee happily enough
And in such eyes as ours appear not faults;
But where thou art not known, why, there they show
Something too liberal.   Pray thee, take pain
To allay with some cold drops of modesty
Thy skipping spirit, lest through thy wild behaviour   170
I be misconstrued in the place I go to
And lose my hopes.
Gra.   Signior Bassanio, hear me:
If I do not put on a sober habit,
Talk with respect and swear but now and then,

Wear prayer-books in my pocket, look demurely,
Nay more, while grace is saying, hood mine eyes
Thus with my hat, and sigh and say ' amen ',
Use all the observance of civility,
Like one well studied in a sad ostent
To please his grandam, never trust me more.   180
    Bass. Well, we shall see your bearing.
    Gra. Nay, but I bar to-night: you shall not gauge me
By what we do to-night.
    Bass.   No, that were pity:
I would entreat you rather to put on
Your boldest suit of mirth, for we have friends
That purpose merriment.   But fare you well:
I have some business.
    Gra. And I must to Lorenzo and the rest:
But we will visit you at supper-time.   [*Exeunt.*

SCENE III.   *The same.   A room in* SHYLOCK'S *house.*

Enter JESSICA *and* LAUNCELOT.

    Jes. I am sorry thou wilt leave my father so:
Our house is hell, and thou, a merry devil,
Didst rob it of some taste of tediousness.
But fare thee well, there is a ducat for thee:
And, Launcelot, soon at supper shalt thou see
Lorenzo, who is thy new master's guest:
Give him this letter; do it secretly;
And so farewell: I would not have my father
See me in talk with thee.   9
    Laun. Adieu! tears exhibit my tongue.   Most beautiful
pagan, most sweet Jew! But, adieu: these foolish drops do
something drown my manly spirit: adieu.
    Jes. Farewell, good Launcelot.   [*Exit Launcelot.*
Alack, what heinous sin is it in me
To be ashamed to be my father's child!

But though I am a daughter to his blood,
I am not to his manners.   O Lorenzo,
If thou keep promise, I shall end this strife,
Become a Christian and thy loving wife.   [*Exit.*

SCENE IV.   *The same.   A street.*

Enter GRATIANO, LORENZO, SALARINO, *and* SALANIO.

Lor. Nay, we will slink away in supper-time,
Disguise us at my lodging and return,
All in an hour.
    Gra. We have not made good preparation.
    Salar. We have not spoke us yet of torch-bearers.
    Salan. 'T is vile, unless it may be quaintly order'd,
And better in my mind not undertook.
    Lor. 'T is now but four o'clock: we have two hours
To furnish us.

Enter LAUNCELOT, *with a letter.*

                Friend Launcelot, what 's the news?
    Laun. An it shall please you to break up this, it shall seem
to signify.   11
    Lor. I know the hand: in faith, 't is a fair hand;
And whiter than the paper it writ on
Is the fair hand that writ.
    Gra.   Love-news, in faith.
    Laun. By your leave, sir.
    Lor. Whither goest thou?
    Laun. Marry, sir, to bid my old master the Jew to sup
to-night with my new master the Christian.
    Lor. Hold here, take this: tell gentle Jessica
I will not fail her; speak it privately.   20
Go.—Gentlemen,   [*Exit Launcelot.*
Will you prepare you for this masque to-night?
I am provided of a torch-bearer.

Salar. Ay, marry, I 'll be gone about it straight.
Salan. And so will I.
Lor.   Meet me and Gratiano
At Gratiano's lodging some hour hence.
   Salar. 'T is good we do so.   [*Exeunt Salar. and Salan.*
   Gra. Was not that letter from fair Jessica?
   Lor. I must needs tell thee all.   She hath directed
How I shall take her from her father's house,   30
What gold and jewels she is furnish'd with,
What page's suit she hath in readiness.
If e'er the Jew her father come to heaven,
It will be for his gentle daughter's sake:
And never dare misfortune cross her foot,
Unless she do it under this excuse,
That she is issue to a faithless Jew.
Come, go with me; peruse this as thou goest:
Fair Jessica shall be my torch-bearer.   [*Exeunt.*

SCENE V.   *The same.   Before* SHYLOCK'S *house.*

Enter SHYLOCK *and* LAUNCELOT.

   Shy. Well, thou shalt see, thy eyes shall be thy judge,
The difference of old Shylock and Bassanio:—
What, Jessica!—thou shalt not gormandise,
As thou hast done with me:—What, Jessica!—
And sleep and snore, and rend apparel out;—
Why, Jessica, I say!
   Laun.   Why, Jessica!
   Shy. Who bids thee call?   I do not bid thee call.
   Laun. Your worship was wont to tell me that I could do
nothing without bidding.

Enter JESSICA

   Jes. Call you? what is your will?   10
   Shy. I am bid forth to supper, Jessica:

There are my keys.   But wherefore should I go?
I am not bid for love; they flatter me:
But yet I 'll go in hate, to feed upon
The prodigal Christian.   Jessica, my girl,
Look to my house.   I am right loath to go:
There is some ill a-brewing towards my rest,
For I did dream of money-bags to-night.

    Laun. I beseech you, sir, go: my young master doth
expect your reproach.   20

    Shy. So do I his.

    Laun. And they have conspired together, I will not say
you shall see a masque; but if you do, then it was not for
nothing that my nose fell a-bleeding on Black-Monday last
at six o'clock i' the morning, falling out that year on Ash-
Wednesday was four year, in the afternoon.

    Shy. What, are there masques?   Hear you me, Jessica:
Lock up my doors; and when you hear the drum
And the vile squealing of the wry-neck'd fife,
Clamber not you up to the casements then,   30
Nor thrust your head into the public street
To gaze on Christian fools with varnish'd faces,
But stop my house's ears, I mean my casements:
Let not the sound of shallow foppery enter
My sober house.   By Jacob's staff, I swear,
I have no mind of feasting forth to-night:
But I will go.   Go you before me, sirrah;
Say I will come.

    Laun. I will go before sir. Mistress, look out at window,
for all this;   40
               There will come a Christian by,
                 Will be worth a Jewess' eye.   [*Exit.*

    Shy. What says that fool of Hagar's offspring, ha?

    Jes. His words were ' Farewell mistress '; nothing else.

    Shy. The patch is kind enough, but a huge feeder;
Snail-slow in profit, and he sleeps by day

More than the wild-cat: drones hive not with me;
Therefore I part with him, and part with him
To one that I would have him help to waste
His borrow'd purse. Well, Jessica, go in: 50
Perhaps I will return immediately:
Do as I bid you; shut doors after you:
Fast bind, fast find;
A proverb never stale in thrifty mind. [*Exit.*
Jes. Farewell; and if my fortune be not crost,
I have a father, you a daughter, lost. [*Exit.*

Scene VI. *The same.*

Enter Gratiano *and* Salarino, *masqued.*

Gra. This is the pent-house under which Lorenzo
Desired us to make stand.
Salar. His hour is almost past.
Gra. And it is marvel he out-dwells his hour,
For lovers ever run before the clock.
Salar. O, ten times faster Venus' pigeons fly
To seal love's bonds new-made, than they are wont
To keep obliged faith unforfeited!
Gra. That ever holds: who riseth from a feast
With that keen appetite that he sits down?
Where is the horse that doth untread again 10
His tedious measures with the unbated fire
That he did pace them first? All things that are,
Are with more spirit chased than enjoy'd.
How like a younker or a prodigal
The scarfed bark puts from her native bay,
Hugg'd and embraced by the wanton wind!
How like the prodigal doth she return,
With over-weather'd ribs and ragged sails,
Lean, rent and beggar'd by the wanton wind!
Salar. Here comes Lorenzo: more of this hereafter. 20

Enter LORENZO.

Lor. Sweet friends, your patience for my long abode;
Not I, but my affairs, have made you wait:
When you shall please to play the thieves for wives,
I 'll watch as long for you then.   Approach;
Here dwells my father Jew. Ho! who 's within?

Enter JESSICA, *above, in boy's clothes.*

Jes. Who are you?   Tell me, for more certainty,
Albeit I 'll swear that I do know your tongue.
Lor. Lorenzo, and thy love.
Jes. Lorenzo, certain, and my love indeed,
For who love I so much?   And now who knows   30
But you, Lorenzo, whether I am yours?
Lor. Heaven and thy thoughts are witness that thou art.
Jes. Here, catch this casket; it is worth the pains.
I am glad 't is night, you do not look on me,
For I am much ashamed of my exchange:
But love is blind and lovers cannot see
The pretty follies that themselves commit;
For if they could, Cupid himself would blush
To see me thus transformed to a boy.
Lor. Descend, for you must be my torch-bearer.   40
Jes. What, must I hold a candle to my shames?
They in themselves, good sooth, are too too light.
Why, 't is an office of discovery, love;
And I should be obscured.
Lor.   So are you, sweet,
Even in the lovely garnish of a boy.
But come at once;
For the close night doth play the runaway.
And we are stay'd for at Bassanio's feast.
Jes. I will make fast the doors, and gild myself
With some more ducats, and be with you straight.
                                        [*Exit above.* 50

Gra. Now, by my hood, a Gentile and no Jew.
Lor. Beshrew me but I love her heartily;
For she is wise, if I can judge of her,
And fair she is, if that mine eyes be true,
And true she is, as she hath proved herself,
And therefore, like herself, wise, fair and true,
Shall she be placed in my constant soul.

Enter JESSICA, *below.*

What, art thou come?   On, gentlemen; away!
Our masquing mates by this time for us stay.

       [*Exit with Jessica and Salarino.*

Enter ANTONIO.

 Ant. Who 's there?   60
 Gra. Signior Antonio!
 Ant. Fie, fie, Gratiano! where are all the rest?
'T is nine o'clock: our friends all stay for you.
No masque to-night: the wind is come about;
Bassanio presently will go aboard:
I have sent twenty out to seek for you.
 Gra. I am glad on 't: I desire no more delight.
Than to be under sail and gone to-night.   [*Exeunt.*

SCENE VII.   *Belmont.   A room in* PORTIA'S *house.*

Flourish of cornets.   Enter PORTIA, *with the* PRINCE OF
MOROCCO, *and their trains.*

 Por. Go, draw aside the curtains and discover
The several caskets to this noble prince.
Now make your choice.
 Mor. The first, of gold, who this inscription bears,
' Who chooseth me shall gain what many men desire ';

 C   (M 330)

The second, silver, which this promise carries,
' Who chooseth me shall get as much as he deserves ';
This third, dull lead, with warning all as blunt,
' Who chooseth me must give and hazard all he hath '.
How shall I know if I do choose the right?   10
    Por. The one of them contains my picture, prince:
If you choose that, then I am yours withal.
    Mor. Some god direct my judgement!   Let me see:
I will survey the inscriptions back again.
What says this leaden casket?
' Who chooseth me must give and hazard all he hath.'
Must give: for what? for lead? hazard for lead?
This casket threatens.   Men that hazard all
Do it in hope of fair advantages:
A golden mind stoops not to shows of dross;   20
I 'll then nor give nor hazard aught for lead.
What says the silver with her virgin hue?
' Who chooseth me shall get as much as he deserves.'
As much as he deserves!   Pause there, Morocco,
And weigh thy value with an even hand:
If thou be 'st rated by thy estimation,
Thou dost deserve enough; and yet enough
May not extend so far as to the lady:
And yet to be afeard of my deserving
Were but a weak disabling of myself.   30
As much as I deserve!   Why, that 's the lady:
I do in birth deserve her, and in fortunes,
In graces and in qualities of breeding;
But more than these, in love I do deserve.
What if I stray'd no further, but chose here?
Let 's see once more this saying graved in gold;
' Who chooseth me shall gain what many men desire '.
Why, that 's the lady; all the world desires her;
From the four corners of the earth they come,
To kiss this shrine, this mortal breathing saint: 40

The Hyrcanian deserts and the vasty wilds
Of wide Arabia are as throughfares now
For princes to come view fair Portia:
The watery kingdom, whose ambitious head
Spits in the face of heaven, is no bar
To stop the foreign spirits, but they come,
As o'er a brook, to see fair Portia.
One of these three contains her heavenly picture.
Is 't like that lead contains her? 'T were damnation
To think so base a thought: it were too gross   50
To rib her cerecloth in the obscure grave.
Or shall I think in silver she 's immured,
Being ten times undervalued to tried gold?
O sinful thought!   Never so rich a gem
Was set in worse than gold.   They have in England
A coin that bears the figure of an angel
Stamped in gold, but that 's insculp'd upon;
But here an angel in a golden bed
Lies all within.   Deliver me the key:
Here do I choose, and thrive I as I may!   60
    Por. There, take it, prince; and if my form lie there,
Then I am yours.   [*He unlocks the golden casket.*
    Mor.   O hell! what have we here?
A carrion Death, within whose empty eye
There is a written scroll!   I 'll read the writing.

[*Reads*]   ' All that glisters is not gold;
                Often have you heard that told:
                Many a man his life hath sold
                But my outside to behold:
                Gilded tombs do worms infold.
                Had you been as wise as bold,   70
                Young in limbs, in judgement old,
                Your answer had not been inscroll'd:
                Fare you well; your suit is cold.'

Cold, indeed; and labour lost:
Then, farewell, heat, and welcome, frost!
Portia, adieu.   I have too grieved a heart
To take a tedious leave: thus losers part.

                [*Exit with his train.   Flourish of cornets.*

  Por. A gentle riddance.   Draw the curtains, go.
Let all of his complexion choose me so.   [*Exeunt.*

Scene VIII.   *Venice.   A street.*

Enter Salarino *and* Salanio.

  Salar. Why, man, I saw Bassanio under sail:
With him is Gratiano gone along;
And in their ship I am sure Lorenzo is not.
  Salan. The villain Jew with outcries raised the duke,
Who went with him to search Bassanio's ship.
  Salar. He came too late, the ship was under sail:
But there the duke was given to understand
That in a gondola were seen together
Lorenzo and his amorous Jessica:
Besides, Antonio certified the duke   10
They were not with Bassanio in his ship.
  Salan. I never heard a passion so confused,
So strange, outrageous, and so variable,
As the dog Jew did utter in the streets:
' My daughter!   O my ducats!   O my daughter!
Fled with a Christian!   O my Christian ducats!
Justice! the law! my ducats, and my daughter!
A sealed bag, two sealed bags of ducats,
Of double ducats, stolen from me by my daughter!
And jewels, two stones, two rich and precious stones,   20
Stolen by my daughter!   Justice! find the girl;
She hath the stones upon her, and the ducats.'
  Salar. Why, all the boys in Venice follow him,
Crying, his stones, his daughter, and his ducats.

Salan. Let good Antonio look he keep his day,
Or he shall pay for this.
    Salar.   Marry, well remember'd.
I reason'd with a Frenchman yesterday,
Who told me, in the narrow seas that part
The French and English, there miscarried
A vessel of our country richly fraught: 30
I thought upon Antonio when he told me;
And wish'd in silence that it were not his.
    Salan. You were best to tell Antonio what you hear;
Yet do not suddenly, for it may grieve him.
    Salar. A kinder gentleman treads not the earth.
I saw Bassanio and Antonio part:
Bassanio told him he would make some speed
Of his return: he answer'd, ' Do not so;
Slubber not business for my sake, Bassanio,
But stay the very riping of the time;   40
And for the Jew's bond which he hath of me,
Let it not enter in your mind of love:
Be merry, and employ your chiefest thoughts
To courtship and such fair ostents of love
As shall conveniently become you there ':
And even there, his eye being big with tears,
Turning his face, he put his hand behind him,
And with affection wondrous sensible
He wrung Bassanio's hand; and so they parted.
    Salan. I think he only loves the world for him.   50
I pray thee, let us go and find him out
And quicken his embraced heaviness
With some delight or other.
    Salar.   Do we so.   [*Exeunt.*

SCENE IX. *Belmont. A room in* PORTIA'S *house.*

Enter NERISSA *with a* Servitor.

Ner. Quick, quick, I pray thee; draw the curtain straight:
The Prince of Arragon hath ta'en his oath,
And comes to his election presently.

Flourish of cornets. Enter the PRINCE OF ARRAGON.
PORTIA, *and their trains.*

Por. Behold, there stand the caskets, noble prince:
If you choose that wherein I am contain'd,
Straight shall our nuptial rites be solemnized:
But if you fail, without more speech, my lord,
You must be gone from hence immediately.

Ar. I am enjoin'd by oath to observe three **things:**
First, never to unfold to any one   10
Which casket 't was I chose; next, if I fail
Of the right casket, never in my life
To woo a maid in way of marriage:
Lastly,
If I do fail in fortune of my choice,
Immediately to leave you and be gone.

Por. To these injunctions every one doth swear
That comes to hazard for my worthless self.

Ar. And so have I address'd me. Fortune now
To my heart's hope! Gold; silver; and base lead.   20
' Who chooseth me must give and hazard all he hath.'
You shall look fairer, ere I give or hazard.
What says the golden chest? ha! let me see:
' Who chooseth me shall gain what many men desire '.
What many men desire! that ' many ' may be meant
By the fool multitude, that choose by show,
Not learning more than the fond eye doth teach;
Which pries not to the interior, but, like the martlet,
Builds in the weather on the outward wall,

Even in the force and road of casualty. 30
I will not choose what many men desire,
Because I will not jump with common spirits
And rank me with the barbarous multitudes.
Why, then to thee, thou silver treasure-house;
Tell me once more what title thou dost bear:
' Who chooseth me shall get as much as he deserves ':
And well said too; for who shall go about
To cozen fortune and be honourable
Without the stamp of merit?   Let none presume
To wear an undeserved dignity. 40
O, that estates, degrees and offices
Were not derived corruptly, and that clear honour
Were purchased by the merit of the wearer!
How many then should cover that stand bare!
How many be commanded that command!
How much low peasantry would then be glean'd
From the true seed of honour! and how much honour
Pick'd from the chaff and ruin of the times
To be new-varnish'd!   Well, but to my choice:
' Who chooseth me shall get as much as he deserves '. 50
I will assume desert.   Give me a key for this,
And instantly unlock my fortunes here.
                                    [*He opens the silver casket.*

    Por. Too long a pause for that which you find there.
    Ar. What 's here? the portrait of a blinking idiot,
Presenting me a schedule!   I will read it.
How much unlike art thou to Portia!
How much unlike my hopes and my deservings!
' Who chooseth me shall have as much as he deserves.'
Did I deserve no more than a fool's head?
Is that my prize? are my deserts no better? 60
    Por. To offend, and judge, are distinct offices
And of opposed natures.
    Ar.   What is here?

[*Reads*] ' The fire seven times tried this:
      Seven times tried that judgement is,
      That did never choose amiss.
      Some there be that shadows kiss;
      Such have but a shadow's bliss:
      There be fools alive, I wis,
      Silver'd o'er; and so was this.
      I will ever be your head: 70
      So be gone: you are sped.'

      Still more fool I shall appear
      By the time I linger here:
      With one fool's head I came to woo,
      But I go away with two.
      Sweet, adieu.   I 'll keep my oath,
      Patiently to bear my wroth.
              [*Exeunt Arragon and train.*

Por. Thus hath the candle singed the moth.
O, these deliberate fools! when they do choose,
They have the wisdom by their wit to lose.   80
  Ner. The ancient saying is no heresy,
Hanging and wiving goes by destiny.
  Por. Come, draw the curtain, Nerissa.

Enter a Servant.

  Serv. Where is my lady?
  Por.   Here: what would my lord?
  Serv. Madam, there is alighted at your gate
A young Venetian, one that comes before
To signify the approaching of his lord;
From whom he bringeth sensible regreets,
To wit, besides commends and courteous breath,
Gifts of rich value.   Yet I have not seen   90
So likely an ambassador of love:
A day in April never came so sweet,

To show how costly summer was at hand,
As this fore-spurrer comes before his lord.
   Por. No more, I pray thee: I am half afeard
Thou wilt say anon he is some kin to thee,
Thou spend'st such high-day wit in praising him.
Come, come, Nerissa; for I long to see
Quick Cupid's post that comes so mannerly.
   Ner. Bassanio, lord Love, if thy will it be! [*Exeunt.* 100

ACT III.

Scene I. *Venice. A street.*

Enter SALANIO *and* SALARINO.

   Salan. Now, what news on the Rialto?
   Salar. Why, yet it lives there unchecked that Antonio hath
a ship of rich lading wrecked on the narrow seas; the Good-
wins, I think they call the place; a very dangerous flat and
fatal, where the carcases of many a tall ship lie buried, as they
say, if my gossip Report be an honest woman of her word.
   Salan. I would she were as lying a gossip in that as ever
knapped ginger or made her neighbours believe she wept for
the death of a third husband. But it is true, without any slips
of prolixity or crossing the plain highway of talk, that the good
Antonio, the honest Antonio,——O that I had a title good
enough to keep his name company!—   12
   Salar. Come, the full stop.
   Salan. Ha! what sayest thou? Why, the end is, he hath
lost a ship.
   Salar. I would it might prove the end of his losses.
   Salan. Let me say ' amen ' betimes, lest the devil cross my
prayer, for here he comes in the likeness of a Jew.

  C 2   (M 330)

Enter SHYLOCK.

How now, Shylock! what news among the merchants?

Shy. You knew, none so well, none so well as you, of my daughter's flight.   21

Salar. That 's certain: I, for my part, knew the tailor that made the wings she flew withal.

Salan. And Shylock, for his own part, knew the bird was fledged; and then it is the complexion of them all to leave the dam.

Shy. She is damned for it.

Salar. That's certain, if the devil may be her judge.

Shy. My own flesh and blood to rebel!

Salan. Out upon it, old carrion! rebels it at these years?

Shy. I say, my daughter is my flesh and blood.   31

Salar. There is more difference between thy flesh and hers than between jet and ivory; more between your bloods than there is between red wine and rhenish. But tell us, do you hear whether Antonio have had any loss at sea or no?

Shy. There I have another bad match: a bankrupt, a prodigal, who dare scarce show his head on the Rialto; a beggar, that was used to come so smug upon the mart; let him look to his bond: he was wont to call me usurer; let him look to his bond: he was wont to lend money for a Christian courtesy; let him look to his bond.   41

Salar. Why, I am sure, if he forfeit, thou wilt not take his flesh: what 's that good for?

Shy. To bait fish withal: if it will feed nothing else, it will feed my revenge; He hath disgraced me, and hindered me half a million; laughed at my losses, mocked at my gains, scorned my nation, thwarted my bargains, cooled my friends, heated mine enemies; and what 's his reason? I am a Jew. Hath not a Jew eyes? hath not a Jew hands, organs, dimensions, senses, affections, passions? fed with the same food, hurt with the same weapons, subject to the same diseases,

healed by the same means, warmed and cooled by the same
winter and summer, as a Christian is? If you prick us, do we
not bleed? if you tickle us, do we not laugh? if you poison us,
do we not die? and if you wrong us, shall we not revenge? If
we are like you in the rest, we will resemble you in that. If
a Jew wrong a Christian, what is his humility? Revenge. If
a Christian wrong a Jew, what should his sufferance be by
Christian example? Why, revenge. The villany you teach
me, I will execute, and it shall go hard but I will better the
instruction.   61

Enter a Servant.

Serv. Gentlemen, my master Antonio is at his house and
desires to speak with you both.
Salar. We have been up and down to seek him.

Enter TUBAL.

Salan. Here comes another of the tribe: a third cannot
be matched, unless the devil himself turn Jew.
                        [*Exeunt Salan., Salar., and Servant.*
Shy. How now, Tubal! what news from Genoa? hast thou
found my daughter?
Tub. I often came where I did hear of her, but cannot find
her.   70
Shy. Why, there, there, there, there! a diamond gone, cost
me two thousand ducats in Frankfort! The curse never fell
upon our nation till now; I never felt it till now: two thousand
ducats in that; and other precious, precious jewels. I would
my daughter were dead at my foot, and the jewels in her ear!
would she were hearsed at my foot, and the ducats in her
coffin! No news of them? Why, so: and I know not what 's
spent in the search: why, thou loss upon loss! the thief gone
with so much, and so much to find the thief; and no satis-
faction, no revenge: nor no ill luck stirring but what lights on

my shoulders; no sighs but of my breathing; no tears but of
my shedding. 82

Tub. Yes, other men have ill luck too: Antonio, as I heard
in Genoa,—

Shy. What, what, what? ill luck, ill luck?

Tub. Hath an argosy cast away, coming from Tripolis.

Shy. I thank God, I thank God. Is 't true, is 't true?

Tub. I spoke with some of the sailors that escaped the
wreck.

Shy. I thank thee, good Tubal: good news, good news! ha,
ha! where? in Genoa? 91

Tub. Your daughter spent in Genoa, as I heard, in one
night fourscore ducats.

Shy. Thou stickest a dagger in me: I shall never see my
gold again: fourscore ducats at a sitting! fourscore ducats!

Tub. There came divers of Antonio's creditors in my company to Venice, that swear he cannot choose but break.

Shy. I am very glad of it: I'll plague him; I'll torture him:
I am glad of it.

Tub. One of them showed me a ring that he had of your
daughter for a monkey. 101

Shy. Out upon her! Thou torturest me, Tubal: it was my
turquoise; I had it of Leah when I was a bachelor: I would
not have given it for a wilderness of monkeys.

Tub. But Antonio is certainly undone.

Shy. Nay, that's true, that's very true. Go, Tubal, fee me
an officer; bespeak him a fortnight before. I will have the
heart of him, if he forfeit; for, were he out of Venice, I can
make what merchandise I will. Go, go, Tubal, and meet me
at our synagogue; go, good Tubal; at our synagogue, Tubal.

[*Exeunt.*

SCENE II. *Belmont.* *A room in* PORTIA'S *house.*

Enter BASSANIO, PORTIA, GRATIANO, NERISSA, *and*
Attendants

Por. I pray you, tarry: pause a day or two
Before you hazard; for, in choosing wrong,
I lose your company: therefore forbear awhile.
There 's something tells me, but it is not love,
I would not lose you; and you know yourself,
Hate counsels not in such a quality.
But lest you should not understand me well,—
And yet a maiden hath no tongue but thought,—
I would detain you here some month or two
Before you venture for me. I could teach you   10
How to choose right, but I am then forsworn;
So will I never be: so may you miss me;
But if you do, you 'll make me wish a sin,
That I had been forsworn. Beshrew your eyes,
They have o'erlook'd me and divided me;
One half of me is yours, the other half yours,
Mine own, I would say; but if mine, then yours,
And so all yours. O, these naughty times
Put bars between the owners and their rights!
And so, though yours, not yours. Prove it so,   20
Let fortune go to hell for it, not I.
I speak too long; but 't is to peize the time,
To eke it and to draw it out in length,
To stay you from election.
    Bass.   Let me choose;
For as I am, I live upon the rack.
    Por. Upon the rack, Bassanio! then confess
What treason there is mingled with your love.
    Bass. None but that ugly treason of mistrust,
Which makes me fear the enjoying of my love:

There may as well be amity and life   30
'Tween snow and fire, as treason and my love.

   Por. Ay, but I fear you speak upon the rack,
Where men enforced do speak anything.

   Bass. Promise me life, and I 'll confess the truth.

   Por. Well then, confess and live.

   Bass.   ' Confess ' and ' love '
Had been the very sum of my confession:
O happy torment, when my torturer
Doth teach me answers for deliverance!
But let me to my fortune and the caskets.

   Por. Away, then! I am lock'd in one of them: 40
If you do love me, you will find me out.
Nerissa and the rest, stand all aloof.
Let music sound while he doth make his choice;
Then, if he lose, he makes a swan-like end,
Fading in music: that the comparison
May stand more proper, my eye shall be the stream
And watery death-bed for him. He may win;
And what is music then? Then music is
Even as the flourish when true subjects bow
To a new-crowned monarch: such it is   50
As are those dulcet sounds in break of day
That creep into the dreaming bridegroom's ear
And summon him to marriage. Now he goes,
With no less presence, but with much more love,
Than young Alcides, when he did redeem
The virgin tribute paid by howling Troy
To the sea-monster: I stand for sacrifice;
The rest aloof are the Dardanian wives,
With bleared visages, come forth to view
The issue of the exploit. Go, Hercules!   60
Live thou, I live: with much much more dismay
I view the fight than thou that makest the fray.

Music, whilst BASSANIO *comments on the caskets to himself.*

.SONG.

Tell me where is fancy bred,
 Or in the heart or in the head?
 How begot, how nourished?
   Reply, reply.
 It is engender'd in the eyes,
 With gazing fed; and fancy dies
 In the cradle where it lies.
   Let us all ring fancy's knell: 70
   I 'll begin it,—Ding, dong, bell.

All. Ding, dong, bell.

Bass. So may the outward shows be least themselves:
The world is still deceived with ornament.
In law, what plea so tainted and corrupt
But, being season'd with a gracious voice,
Obscures the show of evil? In religion,
What damned error, but some sober brow
Will bless it and approve it with a text,
Hiding the grossness with fair ornament?   80
There is no vice so simple but assumes
Some mark of virtue on his outward parts:
How many cowards, whose hearts are all as false
As stairs of sand, wear yet upon their chins
The beards of Hercules and frowning Mars,
Who, inward search'd, have livers white as milk;
And these assume but valour's excrement
To render them redoubted! Look on beauty,
And you shall see 't is purchased by the weight;
Which therein works a miracle in nature,   90
Making them lightest that wear most of it:
So are those crisped snaky golden locks
Which make such wanton gambols with the wind,
Upon supposed fairness often known

To be the dowry of a second head,
The skull that bred them in the sepulchre.
Thus ornament is but the guiled shore
To a most dangerous sea; the beauteous scarf
Veiling an Indian beauty; in a word,
The seeming truth which cunning times put on   100
To entrap the wisest. Therefore, thou gaudy gold,
Hard food for Midas, I will none of thee;
Nor none of thee, thou pale and common drudge
'Tween man and man: but thou, thou meagre lead,
Which rather threatenest than dost promise aught,
Thy paleness moves me more than eloquence;
And here choose I: joy be the consequence!

   Por. [*Aside*] How all the other passions fleet to air,
As doubtful thoughts, and rash-embraced despair,
And shuddering fear, and green-eyed jealousy!   110
O love, be moderate; allay thy ecstasy;
In measure rain thy joy; scant this excess.
I feel too much thy blessing: make it less,
For fear I surfeit.

   Bass.   What find I here?

                [*Opening the leaden casket.*

Fair Portia's counterfeit! What demi-god
Hath come so near creation? Move these eyes?
Or whether, riding on the balls of mine,
Seem they in motion? Here are sever'd lips,
Parted with sugar breath: so sweet a bar
Should sunder such sweet friends. Here in her hairs   120
The painter plays the spider and hath woven
A golden mesh to entrap the hearts of men
Faster than gnats in cobwebs: but her eyes,—
How could he see to do them? having made one,
Methinks it should have power to steal both his
And leave itself unfurnish'd. Yet look, how far
The substance of my praise doth wrong this shadow.

In underprizing it, so far this shadow
Doth limp behind the substance. Here 's the scroll,   130
The continent and summary of my fortune.

> [*Reads*] 'You that choose not by the view,
>   Chance as fair and choose as true!
>   Since this fortune falls to you,
>   Be content and seek no new.
>   If you be well pleased with this
>   And hold your fortune for your bliss,
>   Turn you where your lady is
>   And claim her with a loving kiss.'

A gentle scroll. Fair lady, by your leave;   140
I come by note, to give and to receive.
Like one of two contending in a prize,
That thinks he hath done well in people's eyes,
Hearing applause and universal shout,
Giddy in spirit, still gazing in a doubt
Whether those peals of praise be his or no;
So, thrice-fair lady, stand I, even so;
As doubtful whether what I see be true,
Until confirm'd, sign'd, ratified by you.
    Por. You see me, Lord Bassanio, where I stand,   150
Such as I am: though for myself alone
I would not be ambitious in my wish,
To wish myself much better; yet, for you
I would be trebled twenty times myself;
A thousand times more fair, ten thousand times
More rich;
That only to stand high in your account,
I might in virtues, beauties, livings, friends.
Exceed account; but the full sum of me
Is sum of something, which, to term in gross,   160
Is an unlesson'd girl, unschool'd, unpractised;
Happy in this, she is not yet so old

But she may learn; happier then in this,
She is not bred so dull but she can learn;
Happiest of all in that her gentle spirit
Commits itself to yours to be directed,
As from her lord, her governor, her king.
Myself and what is mine to you and yours
Is now converted: but now I was the lord
Of this fair mansion, master of my servants,   170
Queen o'er myself; and even now, but now,
This house, these servants and this same myself
Are yours, my lord: I give them with this ring;
Which when you part from, lose, or give away,
Let it presage the ruin of your love
And be my vantage to exclaim on you.

   Bass. Madam, you have bereft me of all words,
Only my blood speaks to you in my veins;
And there is such confusion in my powers,
As, after some oration fairly spoke   180
By a beloved prince, there doth appear
Among the buzzing pleased multitude;
Where every something, being blent together,
Turns to a wild of nothing, save of joy,
Express'd and not express'd. But when this ring
Parts from this finger, then parts life from hence:
O, then be bold to say Bassanio's dead!

   Ner. My lord and lady, it is now our time,
That have stood by and seen our wishes prosper,
To cry, good joy: good joy, my lord and lady!   190

   Gra. My lord Bassanio and my gentle lady,
I wish you all the joy that you can wish;
For I am sure you can wish none from me:
And when your honours mean to solemnize
The bargain of your faith, I do beseech you,
Even at that time I may be married too.

   Bass. With all my heart, so thou canst get a wife.

Gra. I thank your lordship, you have got me one.
My eyes, my lord, can look as swift as yours:
You saw the mistress, I beheld the maid;   200
You loved, I loved; for intermission
No more pertains to me, my lord, than you.
Your fortune stood upon the casket there,
And so did mine too, as the matter falls;
For wooing here until I sweat again,
And swearing till my very roof was dry
With oaths of love, at last, if promise last,
I got a promise of this fair one here
To have her love, provided that your fortune
Achieved her mistress.

Por.   Is this true, Nerissa?   210

Ner. Madam, it is, so you stand pleased withal.

Bass. And do you, Gratiano, mean good faith?

Gra. Yes, faith, my lord.

Bass. Our feast shall be much honour'd in your marriage.
But who comes here? Lorenzo and his infidel?
What, and my old Venetian friend Salanio?

Enter LORENZO, JESSICA, *and* SALANIO, *a Messenger
from Venice*

Bass. Lorenzo and Salanio, welcome hither;
If that the youth of my new interest here
Have power to bid you welcome. By your leave,
I bid my very friends and countrymen,   220
Sweet Portia, welcome.

Por.   So do I, my lord:
They are entirely welcome.

Lor. I thank your honour. For my part, my lord,
My purpose was not to have seen you here;
But meeting with Salanio by the way,
He did intreat me, past all saying nay,
To come with him along.

Salan.   I did, my lord;
And I have reason for it. Signior Antonio
Commends him to you.   [*Gives Bassanio a letter.*
    Bass.   Ere I ope his letter,
I pray you, tell me how my good friend doth.   230
    Salan. Not sick, my lord, unless it be in mind;
Nor well, unless in mind: his letter there
Will show you his estate.
    Gra. Nerissa, cheer yon stranger; bid her welcome.
Your hand, Salanio: what' s the news from Venice?
How doth that royal merchant, good Antonio?
I know he will be glad of our success;
We are the Jasons, we have won the fleece.
    Salan. I would you had won the fleece that he hath lost.
    Por. There are some shrewd contents in yon same paper,
That steals the colour from Bassanio's cheek: 241
Some dear friend dead; else nothing in the world
Could turn so much the constitution
Of any constant man. What, worse and worse!
With leave, Bassanio; I am half yourself,
And I must freely have the half of anything
That this same paper brings you.
    Bass.   O sweet Portia,
Here are a few of the unpleasant'st words
That ever blotted paper! Gentle lady,
When I did first impart my love to you,   250
I freely told you, all the wealth I had
Ran in my veins, I was a gentleman;
And then I told you true: and yet, dear lady,
Rating myself at nothing, you shall see
How much I was a braggart. When I told you
My state was nothing, I should then have told you
That I was worse than nothing; for, indeed,
I have engaged myself to a dear friend,
Engaged my friend to his mere enemy,

To feed my means. Here is a letter, lady;   260
The paper as the body of my friend,
And every word in it a gaping wound,
Issuing life-blood. But is it true, Salanio?
Have all his ventures fail'd? What, not one hit?
From Tripolis, from Mexico and England,
From Lisbon, Barbary and India?
And not one vessel 'scape the dreadful touch
Of merchant-marring rocks?
   Salan.   Not one, my lord.
Besides, it should appear, that if he had
The present money to discharge the Jew,   270
He would not take it. Never did I know
A creature, that did bear the shape of man,
So keen and greedy to confound a man:
He plies the duke at morning and at night,
And doth impeach the freedom of the state,
If they deny him justice: twenty merchants,
The duke himself, and the magnificoes
Of greatest port, have all persuaded with him;
But none can drive him from the envious plea
Of forfeiture, of justice and his bond.   280
   Jes. When I was with him I have heard him swear
To Tubal and to Chus, his countrymen,
That he would rather have Antonio's flesh
Than twenty times the value of the sum
That he did owe him: and I know, my lord,
If law, authority and power deny not,
It will go hard with poor Antonio.
   Por. Is it your dear friend that is thus in trouble?
   Bass. The dearest friend to me, the kindest man,
The best-condition'd and unwearied spirit   290
In doing courtesies, and one in whom
The ancient Roman honour more appears
Than any that draws breath in Italy.

Por. What sum owes he the Jew?

Bass. For me three thousand ducats.

Por.   What, no more?

Pay him six thousand, and deface the bond;

Double six thousand, and then treble that,

Before a friend of this description

Shall lose a hair through Bassanio's fault.

First go with me to church and call me wife,   300

And then away to Venice to your friend;

For never shall you lie by Portia's side

With an unquiet soul. You shall have gold

To pay the petty debt twenty times over:

When it is paid, bring your true friend along.

My maid Nerissa and myself meantime

Will live as maids and widows. Come, away!

For you shall hence upon your wedding-day:

Bid your friends welcome, show a merry cheer:

Since you are dear bought, I will love you dear.   310

But let me hear the letter of your friend.

Bass. [*Reads*] Sweet Bassanio, my ships have all miscarried,
my creditors grow cruel, my estate is very low, my bond to
the Jew is forfeit; and since in paying it, it is impossible I
should live, all debts are cleared between you and I. If I
might but see you at my death—notwithstanding, use your
pleasure: if your love do not persuade you to come, let not
my letter.

Por. O love, dispatch all business, and be gone!

Bass. Since I have your good leave to go away,   320

I will make haste: but, till I come again,

No bed shall e'er be guilty of my stay,

No rest be interposer 'twixt us twain.   [*Exeunt*

SCENE III. *Venice. A street.*

Enter SHYLOCK, SALARINO, ANTONIO, *and* Gaoler.

Shy. Gaoler, look to him: tell not me of mercy;
This is the fool that lent out money gratis:
Gaoler, look to him.

Ant.   Hear me yet, good Shylock.

Shy. I 'll have my bond; speak not against my bond:
I have sworn an oath that I will have my bond.
Thou call'dst me dog before thou hadst a cause;
But, since I am a dog, beware my fangs:
The duke shall grant me justice. I do wonder,
Thou naughty gaoler, that thou art so fond
To come abroad with him at his request.   10

Ant. I pray thee, hear me speak.

Shy. I 'll have my bond; I will not hear thee speak;
I 'll have my bond; and therefore speak no more.
I 'll not be made a soft and dull-eyed fool,
To shake the head, relent, and sigh, and yield
To Christian intercessors. Follow not;
I 'll have no speaking: I will have my bond.   [*Exit.*

Salar. It is the most impenetrable cur
That ever kept with men.

Ant.   Let him alone:
I 'll follow him no more with bootless prayers.   20
He seeks my life; his reason well I know:
I oft deliver'd from his forfeitures
Many that have at times made moan to me;
Therefore he hates me.

Salar.   I am sure the duke
Will never grant this forfeiture to hold.

Ant. The duke cannot deny the course of law,
For the commodity that strangers have
With us in Venice. If it be denied,
'T will much impeach the justice of his state:

Since that the trade and profit of the city   30
Consisteth of all nations. Therefore, go:
These griefs and losses have so bated me,
That I shall hardly spare a pound of flesh
To-morrow to my bloody creditor.
Well, gaoler, on. Pray God, Bassanio come
To see me pay his debt, and then I care not!   [*Exeunt.*

SCENE IV. *Belmont. A room in* PORTIA'S *house.*

Enter PORTIA, NERISSA, LORENZO, JESSICA, *and*
BALTHASAR.

Lor. Madam, although I speak it in your presence,
You have a noble and a true conceit
Of god-like amity; which appears most strongly
In bearing thus the absence of your lord.
But if you knew to whom you show this honour,
How true a gentleman you send relief,
How dear a lover of my lord your husband,
I know you would be prouder of the work
Than customary bounty can enforce you.

Por. I never did repent for doing good,   10
Nor shall not now: for in companions
That do converse and waste the time together,
Whose souls do bear an equal yoke of love,
There must be needs a like proportion
Of lineaments, of manners and of spirit;
Which makes me think that this Antonio,
Being the bosom lover of my lord,
Must needs be like my lord. If it be so,
How little is the cost I have bestow'd
In purchasing the semblance of my soul   20
From out the state of hellish misery!
This comes too near the praising of myself;

Therefore no more of it: hear other things.
Lorenzo, I commit into your hands
The husbandry and manage of my house
Until my lord's return: for mine own part,
I have toward heaven breathed a secret vow
To live in prayer and contemplation,
Only attended by Nerissa here,
Until her husband and my lord's return: 30
There is a monastery two miles off;
And there will we abide. I do desire you
Not to deny this imposition;
The which my love and some necessity
Now lays upon you.
    Lor.   Madam, with all my heart;
I shall obey you in all fair commands.
    Por. My people do already know my mind,
And will acknowledge you and Jessica
In place of Lord Bassanio and myself.
And so farewell, till we shall meet again. 40
    Lor. Fair thoughts and happy hours attend on you!
    Jes. I wish your ladyship all heart's content.
    Por. I thank you for your wish, and am well pleased
To wish it back on you: fare you well, Jessica.
                              [*Exeunt Jessica and Lorenzo.*
Now, Balthasar,
As I have ever found thee honest-true,
So let me find thee still. Take this same letter,
And use thou all the endeavour of a man
In speed to Padua: see thou render this
Into my cousin's hand, Doctor Bellario; 50
And, look, what notes and garments he doth give thee,
Bring them, I pray thee, with imagined speed
Unto the traject, to the common ferry
Which trades to Venice. Waste no time in words,
But get thee gone: I shall be there before thee.

Balth. Madam, I go with all convenient speed.   [*Exit.*

Por. Come on, Nerissa; I have work in hand
That you yet know not of: we 'll see our husbands
Before they think of us.

Ner.   Shall they see us?

Por. They shall, Nerissa; but in such a habit,   60
That they shall think we are accomplished
With that we lack. I 'll hold thee any wager,
When we are both accoutred like young men,
I 'll prove the prettier fellow of the two,
And wear my dagger with the braver grace,
And speak between the change of man and boy
With a reed voice, and turn two mincing steps
Into a manly stride, and speak of frays
Like a fine bragging youth, and tell quaint lies,
How honourable ladies sought my love,   70
Which I denying, they fell sick and died;
I could not do withal; then I 'll repent,
And wish, for all that, that I had not kill'd them;
And twenty of these puny lies I 'll tell,
That men shall swear I have discontinued school
Above a twelvemonth. I have within my mind
A thousand raw tricks of these bragging Jacks,
Which I will practise.
But come, I 'll tell thee all my whole device
When I am in my coach, which stays for us   80
At the park gate; and therefore haste away,
For we must measure twenty miles to-day.   [*Exeunt.*

SCENE V. *The same. A garden.*

Enter LAUNCELOT *and* JESSICA.

Laun. Yes, truly; for, look you, the sins of the father are
to be laid upon the children: therefore, I promise ye, I fear
you. I was always plain with you, and so now I speak my

agitation of the matter: therefore be of good cheer, for truly I think you are damned.

Jes. I shall be saved by my husband; he hath made me a Christian.

Laun. Truly, the more to blame he: we were Christians enow before: e'en as many as could well live, one by another. This making of Christians will raise the price of hogs: if we grow all to be pork-eaters, we shall not shortly have a rasher on the coals for money.   12

Enter LORENZO

Jes. I 'll tell my husband, Launcelot, what you say: here he comes.

Lor. I shall grow jealous of you shortly, Launcelot, if you thus get my wife into corners.

Jes. Nay, you need not fear us, Lorenzo: Launcelot and I are out. He tells me flatly, there is no mercy for me in heaven, because I am a Jew's daughter: and he says, you are no good member of the commonwealth, for in converting Jews to Christians, you raise the price of pork.   21

Lor. How every fool can play upon the word! I think the best grace of wit will shortly turn into silence, and discourse grow commendable in none only but parrots. Go in, sirrah; bid them prepare for dinner.

Laun. That is done, sir; they have all stomachs.

Lor. Goodly Lord, what a wit-snapper are you! then bid them prepare dinner.

Laun. That is done too, sir; only ' cover ' is the word.

Lor. Will you cover then, sir?   30

Laun. Not so, sir, neither; I know my duty.

Lor. Yet more quarrelling with occasion! Wilt thou show the whole wealth of thy wit in an instant? I pray thee, understand a plain man in his plain meaning: go to thy fellows; bid them cover the table, serve in the meat, and we will come in to dinner.

Laun. For the table, sir, it shall be served in; for the meat, sir, it shall be covered; for your coming in to dinner, sir, why, let it be as humours and conceits shall govern.   [*Exit.*

Lor. O dear discretion, how his words are suited!   40
The fool hath planted in his memory
An army of good words; and I do know
A many fools, that stand in better place,
Garnish'd like him, that for a tricksy word
Defy the matter. How cheer'st thou, Jessica?
And now, good sweet, say thy opinion,
How dost thou like the Lord Bassanio's wife?

Jes. Past all expressing. It is very meet
The Lord Bassanio live an upright life;
For, having such a blessing in his lady,   50
He finds the joys of heaven here on earth;
And if on earth he do not merit it,
In reason he should never come to heaven.
Why, if two gods should play some heavenly match
And on the wager lay two earthly women,
And Portia one, there must be something else
Pawn'd with the other, for the poor rude world
Hath not her fellow.

Lor.   Even such a husband
Hast thou of me as she is for a wife.

Jes. Nay, but ask my opinion too of that.   60

Lor. I will anon: first, let us go to dinner.

Jes. Nay, let me praise you while I have a stomach.

Lor. No, pray thee, let it serve for table-talk,
Then, howsoe'er thou speak'st, 'mong other things
I shall digest it.

Jes.   Well, I 'll set you forth.   [*Exeunt*

ACT IV.

Scene I. *Venice. A court of justice.*

Enter the Duke, *the* Magnificoes, Antonio, Bassanio, Gratiano, Salanio, *and others.*

Duke. What, is Antonio here?

Ant. Ready, so please your grace.

Duke. I am sorry for thee: thou art come to answer
A stony adversary, an inhuman wretch
Uncapable of pity, void and empty
From any dram of mercy.

Ant.   I have heard
Your grace hath ta'en great pains to qualify
His rigorous course; but since he stands obdurate
And that no lawful means can carry me
Out of his envy's reach, I do oppose   10
My patience to his fury, and am arm'd
To suffer, with a quietness of spirit,
The very tyranny and rage of his.

Duke. Go one, and call the Jew into the court.

Salan. He is ready at the door: he comes, my lord.

Enter Shylock.

Duke. Make room, and let him stand before our face.
Shylock, the world thinks, and I think so too,
That thou but lead'st this fashion of thy malice
To the last hour of act; and then 't is thought
Thou 'lt show thy mercy and remorse more strange   20
Than is thy strange apparent cruelty;
And where thou now exact'st the penalty,
Which is a pound of this poor merchant's flesh,
Thou wilt not only loose the forfeiture,

But, touch'd with human gentleness and love,
Forgive a moiety of the principal;
Glancing an eye of pity on his losses,
That have of late so huddled on his back,
Enow to press a royal merchant down
And pluck commiseration of his state   30
From brassy bosoms and rough hearts of flint,
From stubborn Turks and Tartars, never train'd
To offices of tender courtesy.
We all expect a gentle answer, Jew.
    Shy. I have possess'd your grace of what I purpose:
And by our holy Sabbath have I sworn
To have the due and forfeit of my bond:
If you deny it, let the danger light
Upon your charter and your city's freedom.
You 'll ask me, why I rather choose to have   40
A weight of carrion flesh than to receive
Three thousand ducats: I 'll not answer that:
But, say, it is my humour: is it answer'd?
What if my house be troubled with a rat
And I be pleased to give ten thousand ducats
To have it baned? What, are you answer'd yet?
Some men there are love not a gaping pig;
Some, that are mad if they behold a cat;
And others, at the bagpipe; for affection,
Mistress of passion, sways it to the mood   50
Of what it likes or loathes. Now, for your answer:
As there is no firm reason to be render'd,
Why he cannot abide a gaping pig;
Why he, a harmless necessary cat;
Why he, a woollen bagpipe;
So can I give no reason, nor I will not,
More than a lodged hate and a certain loathing
I bear Antonio, that I follow thus
A losing suit against him. Are you answer'd?

Bass. This is no answer, thou unfeeling man, 60
To excuse the current of thy cruelty.
  Shy. I am not bound to please thee with my answers.
  Bass. Do all men kill the things they do not love?
  Shy. Hates any man the thing he would not kill?
  Bass. Every offence is not a hate at first.
  Shy. What, wouldst thou have a serpent sting thee twice?
  Ant. I pray you, think you question with the Jew:
You may as well go stand upon the beach
And bid the main flood bate his usual height;
You may as well use question with the wolf 70
Why he hath made the ewe bleat for the lamb;
You may as well forbid the mountain pines
To wag their high tops and to make no noise,
When they are fretten with the gusts of heaven;
You may as well do any thing most hard,
As seek to soften that—than which what 's harder?—
His Jewish heart: therefore, I do beseech you,
Make no more offers, use no farther means,
But with all brief and plain conveniency
Let me have judgement and the Jew his will. 80
  Bass. For thy three thousand ducats here is six.
  Shy. If every ducat in six thousand ducats
Were in six parts and every part a ducat,
I would not draw them; I would have my bond.
  Duke. How shalt thou hope for mercy, rendering none?
  Shy. What judgement shall I dread, doing no wrong?
You have among you many a purchased slave,
Which, like your asses and your dogs and mules,
You use in abject and in slavish parts,
Because you bought them: shall I say to you, 90
Let them be free, marry them to your heirs?
Why sweat they under burthens? let their beds
Be made as soft as yours and let their palates
Be season'd with such viands? You will answer

' The slaves are ours ': so do I answer you:
The pound of flesh, which I demand of him,
Is dearly bought; 't is mine and I will have it.
If you deny me, fie upon your law!
There is no force in the decrees of Venice.
I stand for judgement: answer; shall I have it?   100
    Duke. Upon my power I may dismiss this court,
Unless Bellario, a learned doctor,
Whom I have sent for to determine this,
Come here to-day.
    Salan.   My lord, here stays without
A messenger with letters from the doctor,
New come from Padua.
    Duke. Bring us the letters; call the messenger.
    Bass. Good cheer, Antonio!   What, man, courage yet!
The Jew shall have my flesh, blood, bones and all,
Ere thou shalt lose for me one drop of blood.   110
    Ant. I am a tainted wether of the flock,
Meetest for death: the weakest kind of fruit
Drops earliest to the ground; and so let me:
You cannot better be employ'd, Bassanio,
Than to live still and write mine epitaph.

Enter NERISSA, *dressed like a lawyer's clerk.*

    Duke. Came you from Padua, from Bellario?
    Ner. From both, my lord.   Bellario greets your grace.
                              [*Presenting a letter.*
    Bass. Why dost thou whet thy knife so earnestly?
    Shy. To cut the forfeiture from that bankrupt there.
    Gra. Not on thy sole, but on thy soul, harsh Jew,   120
Thou makest thy knife keen: but no metal can,
No, not the hangman's axe, bear half the keenness
Of thy sharp envy.   Can no prayers pierce thee?
    Shy. No, none that thou hast wit enough to make.

Gra. O, be thou damn'd, inexorable dog!
And for thy life let justice be accused.
Thou almost makest me waver in my faith
To hold opinion with Pythagoras,
That souls of animals infuse themselves
Into the trunks of men: thy currish spirit   130
Govern'd a wolf, who, hang'd for human slaughter,
Even from the gallows did his fell soul fleet,
And, whilst thou lay'st in thy unhallow'd dam,
Infused itself in thee; for thy desires
Are wolvish, bloody, starved and ravenous.

Shy. Till thou canst rail the seal from off my bond,
Thou but offend'st thy lungs to speak so loud:
Repair thy wit, good youth, or it will fall
To cureless ruin.   I stand here for law.

Duke. This letter from Bellario doth commend   140
A young and learned doctor to our court.
Where is he?

Ner.   He attendeth here hard by,
To know your answer, whether you 'll admit him.

Duke. With all my heart.   Some three or four of you
Go give him courteous conduct to this place.
Meantime the court shall hear Bellario's letter.

Clerk. [*Reads*] ' Your grace shall understand that at the
receipt of your letter I am very sick: but in the instant that
your messenger came, in loving visitation was with me a
young doctor of Rome; his name is Balthasar. I acquainted
him with the cause in controversy between the Jew and
Antonio the merchant: we turned o'er many books together:
he is furnished with my opinion; which, bettered with his
own learning, the greatness whereof I cannot enough commend, comes with him, at my importunity, to fill up your
grace's request in my stead. I beseech you, let his lack of
years be no impediment to let him lack a reverend estimation;
for I never knew so young a body with so old a head. I leave

him to your gracious acceptance, whose trial shall better
publish his commendation.'   160

 Duke. You hear the learn'd Bellario, what he writes:
And here, I take it, is the doctor come.

   Enter PORTIA, *dressed like a doctor of laws.*

Give me your hand.   Come you from old Bellario?
 Por. I did, my lord.
 Duke.   You are welcome: take your place.
Are you acquainted with the difference
That holds this present question in the court?
 Por. I am informed throughly of the cause.
Which is the merchant here, and which the Jew?
 Duke. Antonio and old Shylock, both stand forth.
 Por. Is your name Shylock?
 Shy.   Shylock is my name.   170
 Por. Of a strange nature is the suit you follow;
Yet in such rule that the Venetian law
Cannot impugn you as you do proceed.
You stand within his danger, do you not?
 Ant. Ay, so he says.
 Por.   Do you confess the bond?
 Ant. I do.
 Por.   Then must the Jew be merciful.
 Shy. On what compulsion must I? tell me that.
 Por. The quality of mercy is not strain'd,
It droppeth as the gentle rain from heaven
Upon the place beneath: it is twice blest;   180
It blesseth him that gives and him that takes:
'T is mightiest in the mightiest: it becomes
The throned monarch better than his crown;
His sceptre shows the force of temporal power,
The attribute to awe and majesty,
Wherein doth sit the dread and fear of kings;
But mercy is above this sceptred sway;

It is enthroned in the hearts of kings,
It is an attribute to God himself;
And earthly power doth then show likest God's   190
When mercy seasons justice.   Therefore, Jew,
Though justice be thy plea, consider this,
That, in the course of justice, none of us
Should see salvation: we do pray for mercy;
And that same prayer doth teach us all to render
The deeds of mercy.   I have spoke thus much
To mitigate the justice of thy plea;
Which if thou follow, this strict court of Venice
Must needs give sentence 'gainst the merchant there.

  Shy. My deeds upon my head!   I crave the law,   200
The penalty and forfeit of my bond.

  Por. Is he not able to discharge the money?

  Bass. Yes, here I tender it for him in the court;
Yea, twice the sum: if that will not suffice,
I will be bound to pay it ten times o'er;
On forfeit of my hands, my head, my heart:
If this will not suffice, it must appear
That malice bears down truth.   And I beseech you,
Wrest once the law to your authority:
To do a great right, do a little wrong,   210
And curb this cruel devil of his will.

  Por. It must not be; there is no power in Venice
Can alter a decree established:
'T will be recorded for a precedent,
And many an error by the same example
Will rush into the state: it cannot be.

  Shy. A Daniel come to judgement! yea, a Daniel!
O wise young judge, how I do honour thee!

  Por. I pray you, let me look upon the bond.

  Shy. Here 't is, most reverend doctor, here it is.   220

  Por. Shylock, there 's thrice thy money offer'd thee.

  S' y. An oath, an oath, I have an oath in heaven:

Shall I lay perjury upon my soul?
No, not for Venice.

Por.   Why, this bond is forfeit;
And lawfully by this the Jew may claim
A pound of flesh, to be by him cut off
Nearest the merchant's heart.   Be merciful:
Take thrice thy money; bid me tear the bond.

Shy. When it is paid according to the tenour.
It doth appear you are a worthy judge;   230
You know the law, your exposition
Hath been most sound: I charge you by the law,
Whereof you are a well-deserving pillar,
Proceed to judgement: by my soul I swear
There is no power in the tongue of man
To alter me: I stay here on my bond.

Ant. Most heartily I do beseech the court
To give the judgement.

Por.   Why then, thus it is:
You must prepare your bosom for his knife.

Shy. O noble judge! O excellent young man!   240

Por. For the intent and purpose of the law
Hath full relation to the penalty,
Which here appeareth due upon the bond.

Shy. 'T is very true: O wise and upright judge!
How much more elder art thou than thy looks!

Por. Therefore lay bare your bosom.

Shy.   Ay, his breast:
So says the bond: doth it not, noble judge?
' Nearest his heart ': those are the very words.

Por. It is so.   Are there balance here to weigh
The flesh?

Shy.   I have them ready.   250

Por. Have by some surgeon, Shylock, on your charge,
To stop his wounds, lest he do bleed to death.

Shy. Is it so nominated in the bond?

Por. It is not so express'd: but what of that?
'T were good you do so much for charity.
   Shy. I cannot find it; 't is not in the bond.
   Por. You, merchant, have you any thing to say?
   Ant. But little: I am arm'd and well prepared.
Give me your hand, Bassanio: fare you well!
Grieve not that I am fallen to this for you;   260
For herein Fortune shows herself more kind
Than is her custom: it is still her use
To let the wretched man outlive his wealth,
To view with hollow eye and wrinkled brow
An age of poverty; from which lingering penance
Of such misery doth she cut me off.
Commend me to your honourable wife:
Tell her the process of Antonio's end;
Say how I loved you, speak me fair in death;
And, when the tale is told, bid her be judge   270
Whether Bassanio had not once a love.
Repent but you that you shall lose your friend,
And he repents not that he pays your debt;
For if the Jew do cut but deep enough,
I 'll pay it presently with all my heart.
   Bass. Antonio, I am married to a wife
Which is as dear to me as life itself;
But life itself, my wife, and all the world,
Are not with me esteem'd above thy life:
I would lose all, ay, sacrifice them all   280
Here to this devil, to deliver you.
   Por. Your wife would give you little thanks for that,
If she were by, to hear you make the offer.
   Gra. I have a wife, whom, I protest, I love:
I would she were in heaven, so she could
Entreat some power to change this currish Jew.
   Ner. 'T is well you offer it behind her back:
The wish would make else an unquiet house.

    Shy. [*Aside*] These be the Christian husbands. I have a
    daughter;
Would any of the stock of Barrabas   290
Had been her husband rather than a Christian.
[*Aloud*] We trifle time: I pray thee, pursue sentence.
    Por. A pound of that same merchant's flesh is thine:
The court awards it, and the law doth give it.
    Shy. Most rightful judge!
    Por. And you must cut this flesh from off his breast:
The law allows it, and the court awards it.
    Shy. Most learned judge! A sentence! Come, prepare!
    Por. Tarry a little; there is something else.
This bond doth give thee here no jot of blood;   300
The words expressly are ' a pound of flesh ':
Take then thy bond, take thou thy pound of flesh;
But, in the cutting it, if thou dost shed
One drop of Christian blood, thy lands and goods
Are, by the laws of Venice, confiscate
Unto the state of Venice.
    Gra. O upright judge! Mark, Jew: O learned judge!
    Shy. Is that the law?
    Por.   Thyself shalt see the act:
For, as thou urgest justice, be assured
Thou shalt have justice, more than thou desirest.   310
    Gra. O learned judge! Mark, Jew: a learned judge!
    Shy. I take this offer, then; pay the bond thrice
And let the Christian go.
    Bass.   Here is the money.
    Por. Soft!
The Jew shall have all justice; soft! no haste:
He shall have nothing but the penalty.
    Gra. O Jew! an upright judge, a learned judge!
    Por. Therefore prepare thee to cut off the flesh.
Shed thou no blood, nor cut thou less nor more
But just a pound of flesh: if thou cut'st more   320

Or less than a just pound, be it but so much
As makes it light or heavy in the substance
Of the division of the twentieth part
Of one poor scruple, nay, if the scale do turn
But in the estimation of a hair,
Thou diest and all thy goods are confiscate.
   Gra. A second Daniel, a Daniel, Jew!
Now, infidel, I have you on the hip.
   Por. Why doth the Jew pause? take thy forfeiture.
   Shy. Give me my principal, and let me go.   330
   Bass. I have it ready for thee; here it is.
   Por. He hath refused it in the open court:
He shall have merely justice and his bond.
   Gra. A Daniel, still say I, a second Daniel!
I thank thee, Jew, for teaching me that word.
   Shy. Shall I not have barely my principal?
   Por. Thou shalt have nothing but the forfeiture,
To be so taken at thy peril, Jew.
   Shy. Why, then the devil give him good of it!
I 'll stay no longer question.
   Por.   Tarry, Jew: 340
The law hath yet another hold on you.
It is enacted in the laws of Venice,
If it be proved against an alien
That by direct or indirect attempts
He seek the life of any citizen,
The party 'gainst the which he did contrive
Shall seize one half his goods; the other half
Comes to the privy coffer of the state;
And the offender's life lies in the mercy
Of the duke only, 'gainst all other voice.   350
In which predicament, I say, thou stand'st:
For it appears, by manifest proceeding,
That indirectly and directly too
Thou hast contrived against the very life

Of the defendant; and thou hast incurr'd
The danger formerly by me rehearsed.
Down therefore and beg mercy of the duke.

   Gra. Beg that thou mayst have leave to hang thyself:
And yet, thy wealth being forfeit to the state,
Thou hast not left the value of a cord;   360
Therefore thou must be hang'd at the state's charge.

   Duke. That thou shalt see the difference of our spirits,
I pardon thee thy life before thou ask it:
For half thy wealth, it is Antonio's;
The other half comes to the general state,
Which humbleness may drive unto a fine.

   Por. Ay, for the state, not for Antonio.

   Shy. Nay, take my life and all; pardon not that:
You take my house when you do take the prop
That doth sustain my house; you take my life   370
When you do take the means whereby I live.

   Por. What mercy can you render him, Antonio?

   Gra. A halter gratis; nothing else, for God's sake.

   Ant. So please my lord the duke and all the court
To quit the fine for one half of his goods,
I am content,—so he will let me have
The other half in use,—to render it,
Upon his death, unto the gentleman
That lately stole his daughter:
Two things provided more, that, for this favour,   380
He presently become a Christian;
The other, that he do record a gift,
Here in the court, of all he dies possess'd of
Unto his son Lorenzo and his daughter.

   Duke. He shall do this, or else I do recant
The pardon that I late pronounced here.

   Por. Art thou contented, Jew? what dost thou say?

   Shy. I am content.

   Por.   Clerk, draw a deed of gift.

Shy. I pray you, give me leave to go from hence;
I am not well: send the deed after me,   390
And I will sign it.

Duke.   Get thee gone, but do it.

Gra. In christening shalt thou have two godfathers:
Had I been judge, thou shouldst have had ten more,
To bring thee to the gallows, not the font.

                                        [*Exit Shylock.*

Duke. Sir, I entreat you home with me to dinner.

Por. I humbly do desire your grace of pardon:
I must away this night toward Padua,
And it is meet I presently set forth.

Duke. I am sorry that your leisure serves you not.
Antonio, gratify this gentleman,   400
For, in my mind, you are much bound to him.

                              [*Exeunt Duke and his train.*

Bass. Most worthy gentleman, I and my friend
Have by your wisdom been this day acquitted
Of grievous penalties; in lieu whereof,
Three thousand ducats, due unto the Jew,
We freely cope your courteous pains withal.

Ant. And stand indebted, over and above,
In love and service to you evermore.

Por. He is well paid that is well satisfied;
And I, delivering you, am satisfied   410
And therein do account myself well paid:
My mind was never yet more mercenary.
I pray you, know me when we meet again:
I wish you well, and so I take my leave.

Bass. Dear sir, of force I must attempt you further:
Take some remembrance of us, as a tribute,
Not as a fee: grant me two things, I pray you,
Not to deny me, and to pardon me.

Por. You press me far, and therefore I will yield.   419
[*To Ant.*] Give me your gloves, I 'll wear them for your sake;

[To Bass.] And, for your love, I 'll take this ring from you:
Do not draw back your hand; I 'll take no more;
And you in love shall not deny me this.

    Bass. This ring, good sir, alas, it is a trifle!
I will not shame myself to give you this.

    Por. I will have nothing else but only this;
And now methinks I have a mind to it.

    Bass. There 's more depends on this than on the value.
The dearest ring in Venice will I give you,
And find it out by proclamation: 430
Only for this, I pray you, pardon me.

    Por. I see, sir, you are liberal in offers:
You taught me first to beg; and now methinks
You teach me how a beggar should be answer'd.

    Bass. Good sir, this ring was given me by my wife;
And when she put it on, she made me vow
That I should neither sell nor give nor lose it.

    Por. That 'scuse serves many men to save their gifts.
An if your wife be not a mad-woman,
And know how well I have deserved the ring,   440
She would not hold out enemy for ever,
For giving it to me.   Well, peace be with you!
               [Exeunt Portia and Nerissa.

    Ant. My Lord Bassanio, let him have the ring:
Let his deservings and my love withal
Be valued 'gainst your wife's commandment.

    Bass. Go, Gratiano, run and overtake him:
Give him the ring, and bring him, if thou canst,
Unto Antonio's house: away! make haste. *[Exit Gratiano.*
Come, you and I will thither presently;
And in the morning early will we both   450
Fly toward Belmont: come, Antonio.   *[Exeunt.*

SCENE II.   *The same.   A street.*

Enter PORTIA *and* NERISSA.

Por. Inquire the Jew's house out, give him this deed
And let him sign it: we 'll away to-night
And be a day before our husbands home:
This deed will be well welcome to Lorenzo.

Enter GRATIANO.

Gra. Fair sir, you are well o'erta'en:
My Lord Bassanio upon more advice
Hath sent you here this ring, and doth entreat
Your company at dinner.
Por.   That cannot be:
His ring I do accept most thankfully:
And so, I pray you, tell him: furthermore,   10
I pray you, show my youth old Shylock's house.
Gra. That will I do.
Ner.   Sir, I would speak with you.
[*Aside to Por.*] I 'll see if I can get my husband's ring,
Which I did make him swear to keep for ever.
Por. [*Aside to Ner.*] Thou mayst, I warrant.
We shall have old swearing
That they did give the rings away to men;
But we 'll outface them, and outswear them too.
[*Aloud*] Away! make haste: thou know'st where I will tarry
Ner. Come, good sir, will you show me to this house?
                                        [*Exeunt.*

ACT V.

SCENE I. *Belmont. Avenue to* PORTIA'S *house.*

Enter LORENZO *and* JESSICA.

Lor. The moon shines bright: in such a night as this,
When the sweet wind did gently kiss the trees
And they did make no noise, in such a night
Troilus methinks mounted the Troyan walls
And sigh'd his soul toward the Grecian tents,
Where Cressid lay that night.

Jes.   In such a night
Did Thisbe fearfully o'ertrip the dew,
And saw the lion's shadow ere himself,
And ran dismay'd away.

Lor.   In such a night
Stood Dido with a willow in her hand   10
Upon the wild sea banks, and waft her love
To come again to Carthage.

Jes.   In such a night
Medea gather'd the enchanted herbs
That did renew old Æson.

Lor.   In such a night
Did Jessica steal from the wealthy Jew
And with an unthrift love did run from Venice
As far as Belmont.

Jes.   In such a night
Did young Lorenzo swear he loved her well,
Stealing her soul with many vows of faith
And ne'er a true one.

Lor.   In such a night   20
Did pretty Jessica, like a little shrew,
Slander her love, and he forgave it her.

Jes. I would out-night you, did no body come:
But, hark, I hear the footing of a man.

Enter STEPHANO

Lor. Who comes so fast in silence of the night?
Steph. A friend.
Lor. A friend! what friend? your name, I pray you, friend?
Steph. Stephano is my name; and I bring word
My mistress will before the break of day
Be here at Belmont: she doth stray about   30
By holy crosses, where she kneels and prays
For happy wedlock hours.
Lor.   Who comes with her?
Steph. None but a holy hermit and her maid.
I pray you, is my master yet return'd?
Lor. He is not, nor we have not heard from him.
But go we in, I pray thee, Jessica,
And ceremoniously let us prepare
Some welcome for the mistress of the house.

Enter LAUNCELOT.

Laun. Sola, sola! wo ha, ho! sola, sola!
Lor. Who calls?   40
Laun. Sola! did you see Master Lorenzo?
Master Lorenzo, sola, sola!
Lor. Leave hollaing, man: here.
Laun. Sola! where? where?
Lor. Here.
Laun. Tell him there's a post come from my master, with
his horn full of good news: my master will be here ere
morning.   [*Exit.*
Lor. Sweet soul, let's in, and there expect their coming.
And yet no matter: why should we go in?   50
My friend Stephano, signify, I pray you,
Within the house, your mistress is at hand;
And bring your music forth into the air.   [*Exit Stephano.*
How sweet the moonlight sleeps upon this bank!
Here will we sit and let the sounds of music

Creep in our ears: soft stillness and the night
Become the touches of sweet harmony.
Sit, Jessica. Look how the floor of heaven
Is thick inlaid with patines of bright gold:
There 's not the smallest orb which thou behold'st   60
But in his motion like an angel sings,
Still quiring to the young-eyed cherubins;
Such harmony is in immortal souls;
But whilst this muddy vesture of decay
Doth grossly close us in, we cannot hear it.

Enter Musicians.

Come, ho! and wake Diana with a hymn:
With sweetest touches pierce your mistress' ear
And draw her home with music.   [*Music.*
    Jes. I am never merry when I hear sweet music.
    Lor. The reason is, your spirits are attentive: 70
For do but note a wild and wanton herd,
Or race of youthful and unhandled colts,
Fetching mad bounds, bellowing and neighing loud,
Which is the hot condition of their blood;
If they but hear perchance a trumpet sound,
Or any air of music touch their ears,
You shall perceive them make a mutual stand,
Their savage eyes turn'd to a modest gaze
By the sweet power of music: therefore the poet
Did feign that Orpheus drew trees, stones and floods;   80
Since nought so stockish, hard and full of rage,
But music for the time doth change his nature.
The man that hath no music in himself,
Nor is not moved with concord of sweet sounds,
Is fit for treasons, stratagems and spoils;
The motions of his spirit are dull as night
And his affections dark as Erebus:
Let no such man be trusted. Mark the music

Enter PORTIA *and* NERISSA.

Por. That light we see is burning in my hall.
How far that little candle throws his beams!   90
So shines a good deed in a naughty world.

Ner. When the moon shone, we did not see the candle.

Por. So doth the greater glory dim the less:
A substitute shines brightly as a king
Until a king be by, and then his state
Empties itself, as doth an inland brook
Into the main of waters. Music! hark!

Ner. It is your music, madam, of the house.

Por. Nothing is good, I see, without respect:
Methinks it sounds much sweeter than by day.   100

Ner. Silence bestows that virtue on it, madam.

Por. The crow doth sing as sweetly as the lark
When neither is attended, and I think
The nightingale, if she should sing by day,
When every goose is cackling, would be thought
No better a musician than the wren.
How many things by season season'd are
To their right praise and true perfection!
Peace, ho! the moon sleeps with Endymion
And would not be awaked.   [*Music ceases.*

Lor.   That is the voice,   110
Or I am much deceived, of Portia.

Por. He knows me as the blind man knows the cuckoo,
By the bad voice.

Lor.   Dear lady, welcome home.

Por. We have been praying for our husbands' healths.
Which speed, we hope, the better for our words.
Are they return'd?

Lor.   Madam, they are not yet;
But there is come a messenger before,
To signify their coming.

Por.   Go in, Nerissa;

Give order to my servants that they take
No note at all of our being absent hence;   120
Nor you, Lorenzo; Jessica, nor you.   [*A tucket sounds.*

Lor. Your husband is at hand; I hear his trumpet:
We are no tell-tales, madam; fear you not.

Por. This night methinks is but the daylight sick;
It looks a little paler: 't is a day,
Such as the day is when the sun is hid.

Enter BASSANIO, ANTONIO, GRATIANO, *and their followers.*

Bass. We should hold day with the Antipodes,
If you would walk in absence of the sun.

Por. Let me give light, but let me not be light;
For a light wife doth make a heavy husband,   130
And never be Bassanio so for me:
But God sort all! You are welcome home, my lord.

Bass. I thank you, madam. Give welcome to my friend.
This is the man, this is Antonio,
To whom I am so infinitely bound.

Por. You should in all sense be much bound to him,
For, as I hear, he was much bound for you.

Ant. No more than I am well acquitted of.

Por. Sir, you are very welcome to our house:
It must appear in other ways than words,   140
Therefore I scant this breathing courtesy.

Gra. [*To Ner.*] By yonder moon I swear you do me wrong;
In faith, I gave it to the judge's clerk.

Por. A quarrel, ho, already! what 's the matter?

Gra. About a hoop of gold, a paltry ring
That she did give me, whose posy was
For all the world like cutler's poetry
Upon a knife, ' Love me, and leave me not '.

Ner. What talk you of the posy or the value?
You swore to me, when I did give it you,   150

That you would wear it till your hour of death
And that it should lie with you in your grave:
Though not for me, yet for your vehement oaths,
You should have been respective and have kept it.
Gave it a judge's clerk! no, God 's my judge,
The clerk will ne'er wear hair on 's face that had it.

Gra. He will, an if he live to be a man.

Ner. Ay, if a woman live to be a man.

Gra. Now, by this hand, I gave it to a youth,
A kind of boy, a little scrubbed boy,   160
No higher than thyself, the judge's clerk,
A prating boy, that begg'd it as a fee:
I could not for my heart deny it him.

Por. You were to blame, I must be plain with you.
To part so slightly with your wife's first gift;
A thing stuck on with oaths upon your finger
And riveted with faith unto your flesh.
I gave my love a ring and made him swear
Never to part with it; and here he stands;
I dare be sworn for him he would not leave it   170
Nor pluck it from his finger, for the wealth
That the world masters. Now, in faith, Gratiano,
You give your wife too unkind a cause of grief:
An 't were to me, I should be mad at it.

Bass. [*Aside*] Why, I were best to cut my left hand off
And swear I lost the ring defending it.

Gra. My Lord Bassanio gave his ring away
Unto the judge that begg'd it and indeed
Deserved it too; and then the boy, his clerk,
That took some pains in writing, he begg'd mine;   180
And neither man nor master would take aught
But the two rings.

Por.   What ring gave you, my lord?
Not that, I hope, which you received of me.

Bass. If I could add a lie unto a fault,

I would deny it; but you see my finger
Hath not the ring upon it; it is gone.
   Por. Even so void is your false heart of truth.
   Bass.   Sweet Portia,
If you did know to whom I gave the ring,
If you did know for whom I gave the ring,   190
And would conceive for what I gave the ring
And how unwillingly I left the ring,
When nought would be accepted but the ring,
You would abate the strength of your displeasure.
   Por. If you had known the virtue of the ring,
Or half her worthiness that gave the ring,
Or your own honour to contain the ring,
You would not then have parted with the ring.
What man is there so much unreasonable,
If you had pleased to have defended it   200
With any terms of zeal, wanted the modesty
To urge the thing held as a ceremony?
Nerissa teaches me what to believe:
I 'll die for 't but some woman had the ring.
   Bass. No, by my honour, madam, by my soul,
No woman had it, but a civil doctor,
Which did refuse three thousand ducats of me
And begg'd the ring; the which I did deny him
And suffer'd him to go displeased away;
Even he that did uphold the very life   210
Of my dear friend. What should I say, sweet lady?
I was enforced to send it after him;
I was beset with shame and courtesy;
My honour would not let ingratitude
So much besmear it. Pardon me, good lady;
For, by these blessed candles of the night,
Had you been there, I think you would have begg'd
The ring of me to give the worthy doctor.
   Por. Let not that doctor e'er come near my house:

Since he hath got the jewel that I loved,   220
And that which you did swear to keep for me,
I will become as liberal as you;
I 'll not deny him anything I have.

   Ant. I am the unhappy subject of these quarrels.

   Por. Sir, grieve not you; you are welcome notwithstanding

   Bass. Portia, forgive me this enforced wrong;
And, in the hearing of these many friends,
I swear to thee, even by thine own fair eyes,
Wherein I see myself—

   Por.   Mark you but that!
In both my eyes he doubly sees himself   230
In each eye, one: swear by your double self,
And there 's an oath of credit.

   Bass.   Nay, but hear me:
Pardon this fault, and by my soul I swear
I never more will break an oath with thee.

   Ant. I once did lend my body for his wealth;
Which, but for him that had your husband's ring,
Had quite miscarried: I dare be bound again,
My soul upon the forfeit, that your lord
Will never more break faith advisedly.

   Por. Then you shall be his surety. Give him this   240
And bid him keep it better than the other.

   Ant. Here, Lord Bassanio; swear to keep this ring.

   Bass. By heaven, it is the same I gave the doctor!

   Por. I had it of him. You are all amaz'd:
Here is a letter; read it at your leisure;
It comes from Padua, from Bellario:
There you shall find that Portia was the doctor,
Nerissa there her clerk: Lorenzo here
Shall witness I set forth as soon as you
And even but now return'd; I have not yet   250
Enter'd my house. Antonio, you are welcome;
And I have better news in store for you

Than you expect: unseal this letter soon;
There you shall find three of your argosies
Are richly come to harbour suddenly:
You shall not know by what strange accident
I chanced on this letter.

   Ant.   I am dumb.

   Bass. Were you the doctor and I knew you not?

   Ant. Sweet lady, you have given me life and living;
For here I read for certain that my ships   260
Are safely come to road.

   Por.   How now, Lorenzo!
My clerk hath some good comforts too for you.

   Ner. Ay, and I 'll give them him without a fee.
There do I give to you and Jessica,
From the rich Jew, a special deed of gift,
After his death, of all he dies possess'd of.

   Lor. Fair ladies, you drop manna in the way
Of starved people.

   Por.   It is almost morning,
And yet I am sure you are not satisfied
Of these events at full.   Let us go in;   270
And charge us there upon inter'gatories,
And we will answer all things faithfully.

   Gra. Well, while I live I 'll fear no other thing
So sore as keeping safe Nerissa's ring.   [*Exeunt.*

NOTES.

Act I.—Scene I.

How Bassanio, a scholar and a soldier, tells the merchant, Antonio, of his purpose to win Portia, the heiress of Belmont; and how Antonio undertakes to find the money to fit out a ship for him.

The early scenes of Shakespeare's plays serve both to introduce the foremost persons of the action, and to give a foretaste of the kind of tale that is to follow. Fine instances of his art in 'overture' are the beginnings of *Hamlet* and *Macbeth*.

Here, we begin by making the acquaintance of the Merchant of Venice himself and of two of his friends, who appear to be courtiers or soldiers. Antonio is out of spirits, and his melancholy is ominous—

> "By a divine instinct men's minds mistrust
> Ensuing dangers" (*Richard III.*, ii. 3. 42).

His anxious words, together with the description by the others of a merchant's risks, suggest the coming trouble. At the same time their solicitude and kindness are prompted by a touch of the same loyal friendship by which that trouble is to be remedied.

Later, we are also introduced to Bassanio and certain of his companions. Immediately upon this the threefold action of the plot begins with Bassanio's story of his hopes of Portia, with Lorenzo's agreement to meet Bassanio 'after dinner', and with Antonio's promise to raise money.

8. Scan this line, and note the word which has a different pronunciation from the modern. Compare 'óbscure', ii. 7. 51, 'aspéct', ii. 1. 8.

13. The little ships feel the motion of the waves, and seem to bob and curtsy to the big, steady galleys of Antonio.

15. **had I such venture forth.** Put this expression along with i. 1. 143, "to find the other *forth*", and ii. 5. 11, "I am bid *forth* to supper", and explain the meaning of the adverb.

16. **affections** in Shakespeare's time had a wider sense than in modern English, and included all feelings or emotions; so also in iv. 1. 49.

18. sits. The wind is said to 'sit' in the quarter towards which it blows. So in *Much Ado About Nothing*, ii. 3. 102, "sits the wind in that corner?"

19. roads, parts of the sea where a ship may safely 'ride' at anchor.

28. Andrew, a name for a galley. It is not known whether Shakespeare had any particular ship in mind.

32. touching but, merely touching. There is a similar order of words in line 153 of this scene, and in iv. 1. 272, "repent but you".

50. two-headed Janus, the god of gates and doors, who therefore was figured 'facing both ways', and so is a type of opposite extremes united in a single nature.

52. peep through their eyes, *i.e.* their eyes are 'screwed up', as their faces wrinkle with laughter.

56. Nestor, a proverb for age and gravity. He lived through three generations, and in the third fought with the Greeks against the Trojans.

61. prevented, anticipated; compare the derivation of the verb.

70. dinner-time, *i.e.* about eleven a. m. Compare the passage in *A Description of England* by William Harrison, an elder contemporary of Shakespeare's (p. 105 in *Elizabethan England*, ed. Furnivall, in the *Camelot Series*), "With us the nobility, gentry, and students do ordinarily go to dinner *at eleven* before noon".

71. where we must meet. Lorenzo is already laying his plans to run off with Jessica, with the help of Bassanio.

74. *i.e.* you take the world more seriously than it is worth, and 'lose' it by losing the power to enjoy it. So Robert Louis Stevenson, after Thoreau: "A man may pay too dearly for his livelihood by giving his whole life for it".

77. At its *second* occurrence in the line, 'world' must be read with a different intonation, and be understood with a different meaning:

'I take the world, but as the *world*'.

A fuller emphasis gives quite another colour to a word, as in—

"Love is not *love*
Which alters where it alteration finds",

or

"If it were *done*, when 't is done, then 't were well
It were done quickly".

78. [In what other places does Shakespeare compare life to acting in a play?]

79. Rosalind says much the same: "I had rather have a fool to make me merry than experience to make me sad".
In this passage "play the fool" means 'act the part of clown'.

80. old wrinkles, *i.e.* such as old age produces.

84. **his grandsire cut in alabaster,** that is, like an effigy on a tomb. Alabaster tombs of Elizabethan times may be seen in many churches. There is a noble example of one at Mytton Church in Yorkshire.

90. **entertain,** we should now say 'maintain'. Schmidt quotes "here we entertain a solemn peace" from the first part of *Henry VI*.

91. **opinion of wisdom** = 'reputation for wisdom'.

92. **conceit** has its original meaning of 'something conceived', a 'thought' or 'fancy'. See note on iii. 4. 2.

99. Expand the phrase from the condensed form in which it appears in the text. What passage of the New Testament is referred to?

101. Gratiano accuses Antonio of putting on an appearance of melancholy to establish his reputation for wisdom. There is a curiously exact parallel in Howell's *Instructions for Forreine Travell* (first published 1642, reprinted by Arber), "The Italians are for the most part of a speculative complexion [*i.e.* disposition], and he is accounted little lesse than a foole who is not melancholy once a day".

102. **this fool gudgeon,** a greedy and stupid fish, easily caught, because it will swallow any bait, and not worth the trouble when you have caught it.

108. **moe,** a different word from 'more', and—in old English—differently used. 'Mo' or 'moe' was used of number, 'more' of size; 'mo' was the comparative used for the positive 'many', 'more' for 'mickle' or 'much'. Vide Skeat's *Etymological Dictionary of the English Language*, s.v. 'more'.

124. **something,** used adverbially = 'somewhat', as in line 129.

port = style of living. How does the word come to have this meaning? What other English words contain the same metaphor?

126. **make moan to be abridged,** means 'complain of being cut down'. Cf. note on line 150.

137. **to stand within the eye of honour,** means 'to be within honour's range'. How would you expand the metaphor contained in this phrase into a simile?

140. **school-days.** It is amusing to put together some of the passages in which Shakespeare speaks of school-days and school-boys: *e.g. Two Gentlemen of Verona*, ii. 1. 21, "to sigh like a schoolboy that hath lost his A B C"; *Much Ado About Nothing*, ii. 1. 229, "the flat transgression of a schoolboy, who being overjoyed with finding a bird's nest, shows it his companion and he steals it"; *Romeo and Juliet*, ii. 2. 156:

"Love goes toward love, as schoolboys from their books,
    But love from love, toward school with heavy looks";

and, best known of all, *As You Like It*, ii. 7. 145:

"And then the whining schoolboy with his satchel
    And shining morning face, creeping like snail
    Unwillingly to school".

In *The Merry Wives of Windsor*, iv. 1., a lad named William, who is being taken to school by his mother, is met in the street by the schoolmaster and made to say his ' Hic, haec, hoc' then and there. The whole passage is very curious, and reads like a reminiscence of Shakespeare's own boyhood.

141. **of the self-same flight,** *i.e.* feathered and weighted for the same distance.

144. = ' I put forward this experience of my boyhood, because of the simplicity of what follows.'

For this sense of ' proof' compare *Julius Cæsar*, ii. 1. 21 :

> " It is a common *proof*
> That lowliness is young ambition's ladder".

150. = ' I have no doubt, from the way in which I mean to watch the aim, that I shall either find both or', &c.

In Shakespearean English ' to' with the verb is used in many senses where nowadays we should either use other prepositions, or else a conjunction with a dependent clause. See line 126 above, and 154 below.

153, 154. = ' You only waste time by approaching your friend in roundabout fashion.'

166. **Cato's daughter, Brutus' Portia,** a clear reference to Sir Thomas North's translation of Plutarch's *Life of Brutus*, wherein Porcia says : " I am the daughter of Cato, and wife of Brutus".

It is interesting to see that, some four or five years before the *Julius Cæsar* was written, Shakespeare had this heroine already in his mind. Bassanio's Portia had several of her namesake's qualities, as Plutarch describes them : " This young Ladie being excellently well seen in Philosophie, louing her husband well, and being of a noble courage, as she was also wise", &c.

The *name* Porcia is the feminine form of the ' gentilician' name of M. Porcius Cato, retained by his daughter, in Roman fashion, after marriage.

The spelling Portia is due to the common sixteenth-century substitution of *-ti-* for *-ci-* in the endings of Latin words. [Sir Thomas North spelt it with a *c*.]

171. **Colchos,** more accurately *Colchis*, a country at the eastern end of the Black Sea, whither Jason went in quest of the Golden Fleece. See note on iii. 2. 238.

175. **I have a mind presages me such thrift.** We should insert the relative pronoun before ' presages'. In modern English we omit the relative only when it would be, if expressed, in the *objective* case, as, *e.g.* : ' I cannot find the book I was reading yesterday'.

Take care to put the accent on the right syllable in ' presages'. Scan the line. Under what general rule does the pronunciation of the word come?

Scene 2.

How Portia, the Lady of Belmont, declares her resolution to marry none but the man who should win her in the manner of her father's will; how she speaks of Bassanio; of the departure of certain suitors, and the coming of the Prince of Morocco.

This scene does something more than show us some of Portia's qualities, her insight into men, her wit, and her loyalty to her father's wishes. It shows that the conditions of the 'lottery' are such as to frighten away the fainter-hearted among her suitors, and to constitute some test of true love; and further, that she has already seen in a poor 'scholar and soldier' from Venice, who had visited Belmont in the train of the Marquis of Montferrat, the man whom she would prefer above all others.

For the *dress* in which we are to imagine Portia, see Godwin in Furness' Variorum Edition, p. 387 : "Portia would do her shopping probably at Padua, and would therefore follow the fashions of the mainland". But any sixteenth-century picture of an Italian lady would be near enough.

1. Portia's opening words recall Antonio's. She is not entirely at ease, though for a different reason.

7. There is a play here between two words, spelt and sounded alike, but of different sense and origin. 'Mean', in the phrase 'it is no *mean* happiness' = trivial or contemptible, and is derived from A.S. 'maene', wicked. 'Mean', in the phrase 'to be seated in the *mean*', = middle or moderate, between two extremes, and comes from the French 'moyen', the Lat. 'medianus'.

In line 21 there is a play of another kind, namely, on two different meanings of the same word, 'will', as again in v. 1. 135, 136, on two meanings of 'bound'.

Such 'puns', or plays on words, have nowadays associations with pantomime or farce; but in Queen Elizabeth's time were often used quite seriously (even 'in real life'), as if the similarity in word or phrase pointed to some analogy in the things themselves. For a serious use of a pun, in this play, compare Antonio's words in what he thought was his dying speech :

"And, if the Jew do cut but deep enough,
I'll pay it presently, *with all my heart*".

11. **chapels had been churches**, *i.e.* small churches would have been large ones. The distinction between a chapel and a church originally was that a chapel had no parish belonging to it, while a church had.

17. **Such a hare is madness the youth, to skip o'er the meshes of good counsel the cripple.** *Draw* the emblem suggested by the words, and see if it is not an admirable picture of the idea. How many such 'picture-phrases' there are in Shakespeare's

poetry! Here are one or two instances to start a collection with:
'Pity' is a 'naked new-born babe' (*Macbeth*). "This drivelling
Love is like a great natural, that runs lolling up and down to hide
his bauble in a hole" (*Romeo and Juliet*, ii. 4. 95). "Wither'd
Murder, alarum'd by his sentinel, the wolf" (*Macbeth*).

38. County Palatine. 'County' for 'Count', as often in Shakespeare ('Princes and Counties', *Much Ado About Nothing*, iv. 1. 317).
A 'Count Palatine' was a count holding office in the *palace* of king
or emperor, with almost royal prerogatives in his own 'fief' or
territory. There were three such in England: the Duke of Lancaster,
the Earl of Chester, and the Bishop of Durham. In Germany the
title had at first a general meaning, as above ('palatine' is the same
word as 'paladin'), but was afterwards applied particularly to the
Lords of the 'Palatinate' on the western bank of the Upper Rhine.

40. If you will not have me, choose. Apparently something
is omitted after 'choose', which Portia expresses by a gesture. Perhaps the phrase means, choose your weapon, as for a duel. His frown
conveys a threat.

42. weeping philosopher, a name traditionally given to Hera-
clitus, in contrast to the 'laugher', Democritus.

52. a capering. 'a' in such phrases is another form of the
preposition 'on'. (Cf. abed, alive, afoot.)

60. Latin was still a 'living language', in the sense of a common means of communication, in Shakespeare's time,—a relic of
the days of the Roman dominion in Western Europe, when Latin
was everywhere the language of church and state. Two generations
later than Shakespeare, when Milton was Cromwell's secretary,
Latin was still used in state despatches to foreign courts, and, even
later still, was used by George I. to converse with Walpole.

62. proper = handsome, as in Authorized Version of *Hebrews* xi.
23: "By faith Moses, when he was born, was hid three months of
his parents, because they saw he was a *proper* child".

64. doublet, a garment fitting close to the body from the neck to
the waist; **round hose,** clothes that went from the waist to the
knees, called 'round', because puffed, so as to be globe-like in
shape.

67. Scottish lord. Altered from the reading in the text, which
is that of the 1600 editions, to "other lord" in the First Folio (1623).
What had happened meanwhile in English History to make the
alteration a politic one?

70. Frenchman; referring to the frequent alliances between
France and Scotland against England. **Sealed under,** *i.e.* put his
seal below the Scotchman's, as his surety.

83. Rhenish wine, a white wine like the modern Hock, grown
in the valley of the Rhine.

91. imposition, conditions laid down.

92. Sibylla. The Sibyl is used here as a proverbial type of old age in *woman*, as Nestor in scene 1. for old age and gravity in *man*. Stories are told of various sibyls or prophetesses, but the most famous by far was the Sibyl of Cumæ, who guided Æneas to the under world, and afterwards sold her three books to the Roman king for the same price as that for which she had at first offered nine. She obtained as a boon from Apollo the power to live for as many years as she could hold grains of dust in her hand.

97. in your father's time, seems to imply he had been dead some little while, and strengthens the general impression produced by the play that Portia is older than most of the heroines of Shakespeare. The Marquises of Montferrat were famous in Italy for centuries. Dante saw one in purgatory:

> "the Marquis William,
> For whose sake Alessandria and her war
> Make Montferrat and Canavese weep".
>   —*Purg.* vii. 134, Longfellow's trans.

107. The four strangers. *Four* should be *six*, to be consistent with the rest of the scene. The same mistake is made in both the Quartos of 1600 and also the First Folio, showing that they are not independent authorities for the text. [Compare a similar blunder, made by all the early editions, in v. 1. 49, where "Sweet soul" is— in spite of sense and metre—given to the clown instead of Lorenzo. This mistake can hardly be taken as a safe ground for believing that a revision was made by the author, and two other characters added to an original four. It is only one more instance of inattention to 'minutiæ', on the part of editors and printers.

Scene 3.

How the Merchant of Venice, who had reviled Shylock the Jew for taking interest on loans, is obliged to ask him for money, with which to equip Bassanio for Belmont. How Shylock agrees to lend it, without interest, on forfeit of a pound of the Merchant's flesh.

No more striking proof of the range of Shakespeare's power could be given than the transition from the previous scene to this, from Portia to Shylock. Each picture is superb, but together they produce the strongest possible effect. Note particularly in this scene the touches by which we are made to feel Shylock's intellectual force, and his stiff-necked tenacity of will. The constant reference to Palestine and Scripture, to Rebekah and Jacob, to the publicans, to the temptation and miracles of Christ, seems to charge the lines with recollections of Jewish history, and of the events which both joined and severed Christianity and Judaism. But how these 'abstractions' are living flesh and blood in Shakespeare's Jew!

The 'get up' of Edwin Booth, the famous American actor (quoted, from his own MS., on page 387 of Furness' Variorum Edition), may

help to call up the detail of the picture. "My costume for Shylock
was suggested by one of a group of Oriental figures in a picture by
Gérôme. It consists of a long, dark-green gown, trimmed at the
edge of the skirt with an irregular device of brown colour. A dark-
brown gaberdine, with flowing sleeves and hood, lined with green,
and trimmed as the gown. A variegated scarf about the waist, from
which depends a leather pouch. Red-leather pointed shoes, and
hat of orange-tawny colour. . . . Head gray and pretty bald: beard
of same colour and quite long. Ear-rings and several finger-rings,
one on the thumb and one on the fore-finger; a long knotted staff.
Complexion swarthy; age about sixty."

11. a good man, *i.e.* of substantial or adequate means, commer-
cially *sound.* Bassanio takes the word in the ordinary sense, and
misunderstands Shylock. Its use in commerce is akin to its use in
law, as when we speak of 'a good title', 'a good claim', or contrariwise, 'a *baa* document'.

15. in supposition, *i.e.* dependent on conditions, and not actually in hand.

bound to Tripolis. The word *bound* here has no connection
by derivation with the word in line 4 above, "Antonio shall be
bound". Applied to ships it means 'ready to go', 'fit for sea', and
was in Middle English spelt 'bown', or 'boun', the final 'd' is an
'excrescence'. There is a fine use of the word in *Sonnet* lxxxvi.—

> "Was it the proud full sail of his great verse
> Bound for the prize of all too precious you
> That did my ripe thoughts in my brain inhearse?" &c.

In general, it means 'prepared', 'ready'. Like the word with
which it is confused, it is a past participle, but from an obsolete verb
meaning to 'till' or 'prepare', which also gives us the substantive
'boor' or 'boer'=a farmer.

Tripolis, *not* the city in Barbary in N. Africa (as is clear from a
comparison with iii. 2. 265 and 266), but the seaport in Syria, a little
to the north-east of Beyrout. The *African* Tripolis was chiefly
famous for its pirates, though there was some little trade with it in
oil (for which see a curious tract, by one Thomas Sanders, called
The Unfortunate Voyage of the Jesus to Tripoli in 1584, reprinted in
vol. ii. of Arber's *English Garner*, where illustrations in plenty may
be found of the risks which Shylock speaks of here). The *Asiatic*
Tripolis was on the way from Venice to the East, by the 'Euphrates
valley route'. It was a famous port in Crusading times, and traded
with Venice in glass.

16. the Indies, *i.e.* the *American* Indies, as in Maria's famous
simile in *Twelfth Night*, iii. 2. 85: "He does smile his face into
more lines than is in the new map with the augmentation of the
Indies".

17. The Rialto, the great meeting-place or 'exchange' of merchants, or a bridge connecting the island named 'Rialto' with the St. Mark's quarter of Venice.

18. England. Throughout the fifteenth, and in the early years of the sixteenth centuries, a fleet sailed yearly from Venice for Flanders and England. But this had ceased in the reign of Elizabeth.

21. Pirates. The Barbary pirates were a terror in the Mediterranean down to the bombardment of Algiers by Lord Exmouth in 1816.

25. Shylock refuses to be 'assured' in the conventional sense, and will make certain by his own inquiries. His answer is as characteristic of *his* keenness, as Bassanio's invitation of the Jew to dinner is consistent with *his* light-hearted ways of doing business.

29. Nazarite, for Nazarene, or inhabitant of Nazareth. So in all translations of the Bible down to the Authorized Version of 1611 (see note in Furness' Variorum Edition).

32. Who is he comes here? For omission of the relative, see note on i. 1. 175.

35. a fawning publican. It is the warmth of the greeting which Antonio gives to Bassanio that suggests the *adjective* (compare the lively feeling he shows at Bassanio's departure, ii. 8. 48). The amiability of Antonio stirs Shylock's gall. (So again in iii. 1. 38, "He that was used to come so *smug* upon the mart".) As to the *substantive,* Shylock identifies himself with the Pharisee's contempt for the humble-minded publican in the parable. Or is he thinking of Zacchæus, the publican who gave half his goods to the poor? The word, with all its associations, by a single touch suggests a whole lifetime of hatred for the religion of people who would "eat with publicans and sinners". [References to the New Testament would not be likely in the mouth of a Jew. But they are none the less vividly suggestive to the *audience.* Compare for Shakespeare's method in this respect the note on iii. 2. 275.]

40. upon the hip, a metaphor from a wrestling-bout.

53. rest you fair. Shylock had stepped aside when Antonio entered and greeted Bassanio. He pretends to have caught sight of him now for the first time.

The phrase 'rest you fair' Schmidt explains by supposing 'God' to be understood as subject to 'rest', as in 'God rest you merry', *As You Like It,* v. 1. 65, where 'rest' has the sense of 'keep'.

56. excess, *i.e.* anything over and above the principal.

57. ripe wants, *i.e.* wants that will not bear delay.

75. pilled me certain wands. 'Me' is idiomatic in phrases of this sort, and has the expletive or demonstrative force of such expressions as 'you know', 'look you', 'I'll trouble you', &c. Compare *Macbeth,* iii. 6. 41, and *Julius Cæsar,* i. 2. 267.

88. Another of the many references to the Bible in this play. When was it that the devil 'cited Scripture for his purpose'?

92. oh what a goodly outside falsehood hath, much what Bassanio says in declining the golden casket (iii. 2. 98).

95. beholding, a corruption of 'beholden', the past partic. of the verb 'behold' in the sense of 'to guard' or 'keep', and, meta-phorically, 'to bind' or 'oblige' (like German *behalten*). Other instances of the confusion between -ing and -en are quoted by Abbott, *Shakespearian Grammar*, § 372.

109. 'moneys' is your suit = the object of your petition is moneys. The word is quoted again, in contempt, from Antonio's request. It is *quoted*, and hence the singular verb with it. Or perhaps 'moneys' may be regarded as a collective, on the false analogy of 'riches' (which is a true singular, from French 'richesse'). In support of this compare "thus much moneys" in line 119 below.

There are abundant traces, however, of an Early English third person plural inflection in -s still surviving in Elizabethan English, *e.g.* line 150 below:

"Whose own hard dealings teaches them suspect",

and *Richard II.*, ii. 3. 4, 5:

"These high wild hills and rough uneven ways
    Draws out our miles, and makes them wearisome".

(See Abbott, *Shakespearian Grammar*, § 333.)

124. The superstitious prejudice against the taking of interest arose from a confusion between loans made in charity or friendship and loans made as a matter of business. The prejudice took the form sometimes of a religious prohibition, sometimes of an argu-mentative attack. It is curious that Aristotle, who founded the scientific treatment of wealth by his exposition of the true nature of money, as a medium of exchange, also lent his authority to the quibble that because metal has no natural power of increase, therefore interest is against nature, as if it were mere metal and not power to acquire commodities which the borrower seeks from his creditor.

126. who, if he break. The 'who' and 'he' are to be taken in close connection with one another as making a compound subject to 'break' (= qui si fidem fefellerit). For similar instances of the relative with supplementary pronoun, see Abbott, *Shakespearian Grammar*, § 249, where, however, a different explanation of this passage is given.

134. your single bond, *i.e.* your bond without any other person as security. This proposal seems a concession on Shylock's part, but it is meant to assist his plan for vengeance, since it leaves no second security to be called in in case of Antonio's failure.

138. equal pound, exact pound.

150. dealings teaches, see on line 109 above.

155. **estimable.** We should apply the word nowadays only to *persons*, but in Elizabethan English its use was less restricted. Compare 'varnished', which we now only use of things, applied to persons in ii. 5. 32, and ii. 9. 49.

156. **muttons, beefs** = French 'moutons, bœufs'. The distinction between 'sheep' and 'ox', on one side, as living animals, and 'mutton' and 'beef', on the other, as the same animals brought to table, had not become fixed in Shakespeare's time, whatever be said in the famous passage at the opening of Scott's *Ivanhoe*.

159. = 'And as for my good-will, I beg you not to hurt me by your suspicions.'

164. **fearful guard**, insecure, risky, or perilous guard. 'Fearful' used to mean 'causing fear for' as well as 'causing fear of'.

Act II.—Scene I.

How the Prince of Morocco would undertake the adventure of the caskets, and what the Lady of Belmont said to him.

The stage-direction in the First Folio edition begins "Enter Morochus a tawnie Moore all in white, and three or foure followers accordingly". The picture of the Moorish prince and his train,

"Dusk faces with white silken turbans wreath'd",

encountering Portia is one of the most striking in the whole of the play. The Moorish chivalry had been, in arts and arms, a match for Christendom, and the romance of the Middle Ages is full of such tales as:

> "When Agrican with all his northern powers
> Besieged Albracca, as romances tell;
> The city of Gallaphrone, from thence to win
> The fairest of her sex, Angelica,
> His daughter, sought by many prowest knights,
> Both *Paynim* and the peers of Charlemain";

or of those who

> "baptized or *infidel*
> Jousted in Aspramont or Montalban,
> Damasco or *Morocco*, or Trebisond
> Or whom Biserta sent from Afric shore
> When Charlemain with all his peerage fell
> By Fontarabia".

The Mahometan warriors were still a peril to Europe in Shakespeare's time. Lepanto, where the author of *Don Quixote* lost an arm, was fought in 1571.

This Moorish prince, with his gallantry, passionate feeling, and boyish simplicity, suggests an early study of Moorish character, afterwards worked out in the 'Moor of Venice'. His words have a fine rolling rhythm, his style a Southern gaudiness of colour.

7. *Red* blood, as Johnson pointed out, was thought a sign of courage, while cowards "have livers white as milk" (below, iii. 2. 86).

9. **fear'd** = frightened. The verb 'fear' commonly had this transitive force in Old English, and often in Shakespeare, *e.g. Henry V.*, i. 2. 155:

"She hath been, then, more *fear'd* than harm'd, my liege".

24. **scimitar.** Like Othello's famous sword,

"a better never did itself sustain
Upon a soldier's thigh" (*Othello*, v. 2. 260).

25. **The Sophy**, *i.e.* the Shah of Persia. The Persians were famous swordsmen ; cf. *Twelfth Night*, iii. 4. 307, "he has been fencer to the Sophy".

26. **Sultan Solyman**, called the 'Magnificent', was the tenth Ottoman Sultan, and reigned from 1520 to 1566. He took Belgrade and Rhodes from the Christians, but failed to capture Vienna. He also suffered defeat in Persia about 1534.

32. **Lichas**, the squire or attendant of Hercules, Ovid's *Metamorphoses*, ix. Alcides = Hercules, from the fact that Alcæus was his grandfather.

33. = (to decide) 'which is the better man'.

35. **Page**, one of Theobald's 'emendations'. Quartos and Folios have 'Rage'.

43. **Nor will not**, emphatic double negative = 'No more I will' (speak to lady afterward, &c.).
Scan line 43.

44. **the temple** where the oath to observe the conditions was to be taken.

46. **blest or cursed'st.** The superlative termination to one adjective does duty for both, as below, iii. 2. 290—

"The best condition'd and unwearied spirit",

and *Measure for Measure*, iv. 6. 13—

"The generous and gravest citizens".

(See Abbott, *Shaksp. Gr.*, § 398.)

Scene 2.

How Launcelot Gobbo leaves his master, Shylock, to take service under Bassanio, and how Gratiano obtains Bassanio's leave to go with him to Belmont.

We must suppose some days to have elapsed since the bond was sealed. Meanwhile Bassanio has bought or hired a ship for his enterprise, and is engaged in hiring and clothing a retinue of followers.

Launcelot Gobbo is the 'clown' of the piece. He is a country lad, son of a small farmer, who has a horse called Dobbin, and keeps pigeons. Occasionally the old man comes into Venice to see how his boy is getting on in town-service. Thus Launcelot is not a professional jester like the Fools in *King Lear*, *Twelfth Night*, and *As You Like It*, but a servant by trade, and a wag by humour. His country appetite and power of sleeping, his untiring spirits and broad outspokenness prove him a 'clown' compared to the courtly attendants of Portia.

1. It looks as if there should be a 'not' before 'serve'. (Halliwell.)

14. **grow to**, a 'country phrase', applied originally to milk which, in cooking, has been burnt to the bottom of the saucepan, and so has acquired a taste. (See note in Furness' Variorum Edition.)

21. **saving your reverence** = salvâ reverentiâ, *i.e.* if I may say so without offence.

22. **incarnal.** Launcelot has not got quite the right word here. Compare 'confusions' in 31, 'frutify' in 120, and 'impertinent' in 123. His father has an equal difficulty with words from the Latin, such as 'infection' and 'defect'. 'Malapropisms' of this sort were particularly rife in Shakespeare's time, when new words from other languages, especially Latin, were pouring in to the vocabulary of English. Launcelot's learning, like Ancient Pistol's, smacks of the playhouse, as in his reference to the Sisters Three, to Fortune a woman, and his use of 'via' for away, and 'ergo' for therefore.

30. **sand-blind**, lit. half-blind (O.E. *sám-blind*); but the first syllable was already in Shakespeare's time misinterpreted, as Launcelot's pun shows. Capell's note on the word is: 'That is, purblind'; a vulgar phrase for it, as *stone-blind* is for those who are quite so; Launcelot finds a 'blind' between these, which he calls 'gravel-blind'.

46. **well to live**, according to Furness means 'with every prospect of a long life'. But it seems better to take it as = 'well off', and then the phrase is an absurdity of the Dogberry stamp ("You are thought here to be the most senseless and fit man for the constable of the watch", &c.). Old Gobbo utters just such another in line 63 below.

49. The father refuses to give his son the title 'Master', which the son continually repeats with increased emphasis.

83. **what a beard hast thou got.** The traditional stage 'business' here is that Launcelot should kneel down and present the *back* of his head to his father, who takes the long, thick hair for a beard.

87. **hair of his tail.** A comparison of Launcelot's words with Old Gobbo's shows that 'of' has much the same sense as 'on' here.

E   (M 330)

Abbott (*Shakespearian Grammar*, § 175) quotes *Taming of Shrew*, iv. 1. 71—

> " My master riding behind my mistress—
> Both *of* one horse".

The gradual change from Shakespeare's English to ours is nowhere more clearly marked than in the uses of prepositions. The student should *collect instances for himself* of cases where prepositions are employed otherwise than they would be in modern English.

For ' of ' compare line 67 above, "you might fail *of* the knowing me", with ix. 11, and

> " We have not spoke as yet *of* torchbearers ", ii. 4. 5 and 23.
> " I have no mind *of* feasting forth to-night ", ii. 5. 36.

93. **set up my rest to run away,** to 'set up a rest' was a term in games of chance, and seems to have meant to make a wager over and above the ordinary stake, to ' back one's chance' heavily; and so to 'plunge' on something in a metaphorical sense, to put everything on a single resolve.

Here there is a play on the two meanings of 'rest'. It is an instance of the amazing range of Shakespeare's power that the very same play on words is used with extraordinary effect in one of the saddest scenes in tragedy (written, perhaps, within a short time of **the** *Merchant of Venice*):

> " O here
> Will I set up my everlasting rest
> And shake the yoke of inauspicious stars
> From my world-wearied flesh ".
>
> (*Romeo and Juliet*, v. 3. 109.)

97. **give me your present to one Master Bassanio.** For this use of ' me ', cf. i. 3. 75, where, however, the meaning is not quite the same. Here it = ' for me ', or ' please ', as in

> "Heat *me* these irons hot" (*King John*, iv. 1. 1).

100. **to him, father,** the verb of motion is often omitted in such phrases, especially in the imperative mood. So " Father, in ", in line 141, and in the infinitive mood,

> "I must to Coventry" (*Richard II.*, i. 2. 56).

[The idiom includes far more than an ellipsis after 'will' and 'is', as Abbott explains it in § 405 of his Grammar.]

103. **supper...ready...by five of the clock.** Elizabethan meals and meal-times were startlingly unlike ours. " The nobility, gentry, and students dined at eleven before noon, and supped between five and six. The merchant dined at twelve, and supped at six. Husbandmen dined at noon and supped at seven or eight. To take two meals only was the rule; none but the young, the sick, and very early risers were thought to need odd repasts". (*Social England,* ed. H. D. Traill, vol. iii. p. 392 of the 1895 edition, following the passage in Harrison, cited above, i. 1. 70.)

135. The old proverb, *i.e.* as Staunton pointed out, " God's grace is gear enough ".

parted, *i.e.* divided.

140. more guarded, with more facings or coloured stripes set across it, the mark of a jester; compare the description of a fool in line 16 of the prologue to *Henry VIII.*—

" A fellow
In a long motley coat guarded with yellow ".

143. table, a term of 'chiromancy', the magic art which foretells a person's future from the lines on his hand. 'Table' means the palm of the hand extended.

It is perhaps futile to expect to make exact grammar or sense out of the sentence beginning, "If any man in Italy have a fairer table". The passage is 'corrupt', *i.e.* we have not got the words as Shakespeare wrote them. I believe the sentence contains a reference, which the commentators have missed, to the custom of swearing with uplifted hand in a court of law.

144. a simple line of life; 'simple' is sarcastic of course, 'line of life' is the main line across the hand.

152. During this talk between Launcelot and Old Gobbo, Bassanio and Leonardo have been conversing on one side. They now come forward.

155. hie thee. The 'thee' is reflexively used.

157. The respect which Bassanio's friends have for him appears in the way in which they address him, 'Signior Bassanio' here. 'My Lord Bassanio', i. 1. 69, &c.

163. hear thee, Gratiano. In this case the 'thee' cannot be reflexive, as in 155 above. It stands for 'thou', as in such phrases as 'fare thee well', 'look thee here', 'stand thee by', &c. &c.

In these instances, the pronoun *following* the verb was, by a subtle form of false analogy, put in the accusative case, as Professor Jespersen explains in his *Progress of Language.*

165. Parts, *i.e.* qualities.

168. liberal = 'free' to the point of 'taking liberties'. The word is coupled with 'profane' in *Othello,* ii. 1. 165, and seems to mean 'excessively free-spoken' in *Hamlet,* iv. 7. 171.

182. sad ostent, serious behaviour.

Scene 3.

Of a letter, which Jessica, the Jew's daughter, sent to her lover, Lorenzo, by the hand of Launcelot Gobbo.

10. exhibit. Launcelot has got hold of the wrong word again. See note on line 22 of preceding scene.

17. manners included more in its Elizabethan use than it does

now, and embraced the big rules of life as well as the small ones,—
everything, indeed, which the Romans expressed by 'mores'. Hence
it appears in the sixth of the 'xxxix. Articles' in reference to the
books of the Apocrypha: "And the other books the church doth
read for example of life and instruction of *manners*".

Nothing can quite reconcile us to Jessica's desertion of her father.
He does not seem to have ill-treated her in any way except that he
enforced a very strict and lonely life upon her. Put he had made
himself 'impossible' to her by his absorption in business and his
attitude towards his neighbours.

Scene 4.

*How Lorenzo plans to carry off Jessica, disguised as a page, with
the help of Gratiano and others.*

5. 'We have not bespoken, or ordered beforehand, torchbearers
for ourselves.' 'Speak' for 'bespeak' is like 'fall' for 'befall',
'long' for 'belong', 'friend' for 'befriend', &c. &c., often found
in Shakespeare. (See Abbott, *Shaks. Gram.*, § 460.)

'Us' is the *dative* of the pronoun. For the use of 'of' compare
below, iv. 1. 396—

"I humbly do desire your grace *of* pardon".

6. vile; not in so strong a sense as that in which it is now used;
but rather = 'poor', 'below the mark'. The stronger sense appears
in the next scene, line 29.

7. undertook, for 'undertaken', as 'spoke' for 'spoken'.

10. it shall seem to signify, a pleasant sarcasm on this kind of
correspondence.

22. provided of a torchbearer. Yet another obsolete use of
the preposition, exactly paralleled in *Macbeth*, i. 2. 13—

"Supplied *of* kerns and gallowglasses".

See above note on ii. 2. 87.

31. gold and jewels. It never even occurs to Lorenzo or
Jessica or any of their friends that there was anything to be said
against their going off with Shylock's property. If they *had* thought
about it, they would have defended it on the ground that Shylock
made no use of his wealth, and that he was a common enemy with
whom the ordinary laws did not hold.

36. she do it. *Mis*fortune is personified as a woman, like
Fortune in scene 2.

Scene 5.

*How Shylock goes to sup with Bassanio, and leaves his keys with
'essica.*

2. the difference of. This is a further instance to add to a
collection of Shakespearean uses of this preposition. Here it means

'in respect to', and so, in comparing two persons, 'between'.
Compare—

> "Since my soul . . . could *of* men distinguish"
>
> (*Hamlet*, iii. 2. 68, 69).

Another 'objective' use, of a slightly different kind, comes in line 36
below—

> "I have no mind *of* feasting forth to-night".

3 and 6. What and Why are used as exclamations of impatience.
Cf. *Julius Cæsar*, ii. 1. 1: "What, Lucius, ho!"

12. Jessica's alacrity in taking the keys adds to Shylock's feeling
of uneasiness.

15. Jessica, my girl, look to my house. However much
Shylock inspires hatred and fear, it is impossible to hear him speak
thus without some feeling of compassion. The audience have been
let into the secret of the plot; Jessica and Launcelot are part of a
conspiracy against the Jew, and here he is, committing his keys to
one of them. The whole situation, therefore, is, like Shylock's
words, full of 'dramatic irony'; that is, it bears a very different
meaning to some of the persons present, from that which it conveys
to those who are not in the secret.

**I am right loath to go. There is some ill a-brewing
towards my rest.** A helpless presentiment such as this, does more
than anything to add to the horror and pity of disaster, because we
are inclined to feel 'it might so easily have been otherwise'. So, in
Hamlet, the prince says, just before his fencing-bout with Laertes,
"Thou wouldst not think how ill all is here about my heart: but it
is no matter". When Horatio urges him to pay heed to the presentiment and to put off the fencing, Hamlet answers, "Not a whit,
we defy augury: there's a special providence in the fall of a sparrow:
—if it be not now, yet it will come; the readiness is all"—and so he
goes to his death.

This 'tragic irony' and these fruitless misgivings might have engaged our feelings too much in Shylock's favour but for the grotesque
and grim

> "For I did dream of money-bags to-night".

20. reproach. Launcelot has got hold of the wrong word again.
Shylock takes up his blunder, and accepts it in another sense.

24. Black-Monday, *i.e.* Easter Monday. "In the 34 Edward
III. (1360), the 14 of April, & the morrow after Easter-day, K.
Edwarde with his hoast lay before the cittie of Paris; which day
was full darke of mist & haile, & so bitter cold that many men died
on their horses backs with the cold. Wherefore unto this day it
hath been called the Blacke Monday."—*Stow.* (See note in Furness.)

27. masques, a form of amusement which consisted in a number of persons, wearing visors and suitably disguised, going in procession to a house where festivities were on foot, and there acting a short play, or leading an elaborate dance. So in *Henry VIII.*, the king himself takes a number of 'masquers' to Wolsey's supper-party.

29. wry-neck'd fife. Here 'fife' means a player on the fife, as in the third part of *Henry VI.*, v. I. 16, trumpet = trumpeter:

"Go, trumpet, to the walls and sound a parle".

Boswell, cited by Furness, quotes an exact parallel from Barnaby Rich's (1616) *Aphorismes*: "A fife is a wry-neckt musician, for he always looks away from his instrument".

30. clamber. The small old-fashioned window would be high up on the wall, just under the ceiling.

32. varnish'd, painted, or disguised.

35. By Jacob's staff. The reference seems to be to *Genesis* xxxii. 10, where Jacob, on his return from Padan-aram, says, "With my staff I passed over this Jordan; and now I am become two bands".

36. to-night means here the 'coming night', while in line 18 it means the 'night before'.

42. worth a Jewess' eye, worth looking at, to a Jewess. Launcelot puns on the old proverb, 'Worth a Jew's eye', used to express something very precious. The reading of the early editions is "worth a Jewes eye".

43. Hagar's offspring. As a Gentile and as a servant Launcelot is, to Shylock, a child of 'the bond-woman, not of the free'.

46. Launcelot's laziness is so extreme as to stir Shylock's fancy. He compares him to three different animals in two lines.

51. Shylock's suspicion was, in this case, well-founded, but it is suspicion of such a kind and expressed in such a way that 'human' relations had ceased to be possible with him.

54. Notice here the *rhyming* close, frequent in the play. The rhyme not only marks the two 'exits', but also the proverbial or epigrammatic sayings with which father and daughter take leave for the last time.

Fast bind, fast find, as Shylock's last words to his daughter, are again full of 'dramatic irony'—as much so, in a different way, as old King Duncan's last message from his bed-chamber to Lady Macbeth, his 'most kind hostess'. We are prepared for the frightful shock and convulsion, which the news of his daughter's flight will cause to Shylock. Irving goes the length of introducing a 'dumb-show' scene for which there is no warrant in the text. He shows the old Jew at the end of scene 6 returning after supper at Bassanio's, knocking at the door of his empty house, and staring up in fear and anger when no answer comes.

Scene 6.

How Lorenzo, helped by Gratiano and Salarino, runs away with the miser's daughter in the disguise of a page.

5. Venus' pigeons, the doves that drew the airy chariot of Venus.

7. obliged, be careful to sound the -ed in reading this and similar lines, *e.g.* lines 13 and 16. The word here signifies 'pledged previously'.

10. = What horse retraces a long distance with the same spirit with which he first traversed it?
There is no need to suppose any reference here to a 'performing' or 'dancing horse'. The saying is applicable to any horse which has a long distance to go and come back.

14. The simile is a striking one, all the more too that it is in harmony with a main 'motive' of the play. **Scarfed bark** is a vivid phrase for a fresh-trimmed vessel, wearing her sails like so much finery.

18. over-weather'd ribs. 'Weather' is here used in the same sense as that in which stone or brick is said to 'weather', *i.e.* change shape and colour.

24. Scan the line. What irregularity of metre is there, and how is it to be explained?

26. Enter Jessica, above, *i.e.* in a balcony.

30. who love I. "The inflection of *who* is frequently neglected. Cf. 'Who I myself struck down', *Macbeth*, iii. 1. 123" (Abbott, *Shakesp. Gram.*, § 274).

42. too light, a play between 'light', meaning 'bright', and 'light' meaning 'frivolous', as in v. 1. 129:

"Let me give light, but let me not be light;
For a light wife doth make a heavy husband".

43. office of discovery, *i.e.* the duty of a torch-bearer is to show things up.

47. The close night, the secret or concealing night. So the witches in *Macbeth* are called "close contrivers of all harms".

65. presently, not in its modern sense, but 'immediately'. Generations of unpunctuality have weakened the force of the word, cf. ii. 9. 3. And compare the similar change of meaning in 'anon', 'just now', 'by and by', 'soon'.

67. I am glad on't. Here 'on' is interchangeable in usage with 'of', as actually found above, ii. 2. 85 and 87. Abbott (*Shakes. Gram.*, § 181) cites:

"God ha' mercy *on* his soul,
And *of* all Christian souls" (*Hamlet*, iv. 5. 200).

Scene 7.

Of the three caskets, the Prince of Morocco chooses the golden.

3, 4. "who" and "which" used interchangeably, Abbott, §§ 264, 265.

20. A golden mind : 'golden' here has the general sense of 'precious', 'excellent', as elsewhere in Shakespeare, 'golden opinions', 'golden joys', &c.

25. The Moor's good opinion of himself is so honestly and heartily expressed that it is little more than healthy military 'swagger' put into words.

29. = To be doubtful of my own merits would be only a spiritless disparagement of myself.

The feeling is much the same as that in Montrose's famous lines:

> " He either fears his fate too much
> Or his deserts are small,
> Who fears to puts it to the touch
> To win or lose it all".

31. Why that 's the lady. At the first time this phrase occurs all the emphasis is on '*lady*'. Lower down, on line 38, it is on '*that's*'.

38. The rhythm of the speech changes from the broken style of indecision to a rapid and continuous flow of excited eloquence. The generous Moor loses the thought of his own merits in the picture, which his mind's eye calls up, of the universal pilgrimage to the shrine of Portia.

40. Mortal breathing, opposed to the sculptured figures of the saints to be found at most shrines.

41. Hyrcanian deserts, in Asia, south of the Caspian Sea, famous for tigers.

44. whose head spits in the face of heaven. The expression is overstrained and the metaphor forced. Such a phrase is called a 'conceit'. Over-elaborate fancy was a common fault in the style of the Elizabethan Age. Shakespeare often makes fun of it (*e.g.* below, ii. 9. 97), but he also is sometimes guilty of it himself. This play, however, is singularly free from 'conceits'. It is quite in keeping that the Prince of Morocco should use them.

50. = It would be too common to inclose her shroud in the darkness of the grave (see Glossary for the words).

53. being undervalued, that is 'silver', not 'she'. The 'ratio' of value between gold and silver in Shakespeare's time was about 10 : 1. Since then silver has greatly 'depreciated'.

57. insculp'd upon, *i.e.* engraved on the surface of the coin. Coins of this kind were struck by Edward IV., and were in use from his reign to that of Charles I. They were of gold, containing a

weight of metal that would be valued now at something between
6s. 8d. and 10s. The name 'angel' was given to them from the
figure which they bore of St. Michael subduing the dragon.

64. **a carrion Death**, a fleshless skull.

65. Scan the lines on the scroll. What metre are they written in?

69. **tombs.** The two first Quartos and the First Folio have
'timber', a mistake which Johnson was the first to correct. A similar
blunder in all the early editions occurs, ii. 1. 35 (where see note).
For the inference to be made from such a 'state of the text' see
Appendix on the Text.

75. **welcome, frost.** This is, says Halliwell, an inversion of the
old proverb, 'farewell, frost', used on the departure of anything
unpleasing.

Scene 8.

*How two gentlemen of Venice describe the rage of Shylock at finding
his daughter flown, and the grief of Antonio at the departure of his
friend for Belmont.*

Apparently we are to understand that the choice of the Prince of
Morocco took place on the very night that Bassanio sailed.

From ii. 2 to ii. 7 we seem to be dealing with the events of a
single day. At the opening of the present scene, a night has elapsed
since Bassanio's departure. We hear that Shylock has discovered
Jessica's flight, and has suspected Bassanio of being concerned in it.
We hear also of that for which i. 1 had somewhat prepared us,
namely, of losses of Antonio at sea.

16. **Fled with a Christian**, and so had cut herself off from the
number of the chosen people. Shylock's passion is of a piece with
the convictions which the Jews held, at anyrate after the return from
the Babylonish captivity. So when Ezra heard of the 'mixed
marriages', he says of himself, "I rent my garment and my mantle,
and plucked off the hair of my head and of my beard, and sat down
astonied" (*Ezra*, ix. 3).

27. **reason'd** = talked, its usual sense in Shakespeare.

33. **You were best**, *i.e.* it would be best for you. 'You' is the
indirect object in this phrase, and 'were' an impersonal verb, as
comparison with Anglo-Saxon usage shows. But by Shakespeare's
time the origin of the phrase had been forgotten, and we find such
expressions as "I were better to leave him", "She were better love
a dream" (for "me were", "her were"). See Abbott, § 230, and
note on v. i. 175 below.

37. **some speed of his return.** See note on ii. 5. 2.

42. **in** for 'into', so v. 1. 56: "let the sounds of music creep in
our ears". We still speak of 'falling *in* love'.

mind of love for 'loving mind'; so in iii. 1. 9, "slips of
prolixity"=prolix slips.

45. **conveniently,** suitably.

48. **sensible** = sensitive. The alteration in modern English of
the use of the words 'sensible' and 'sensibly' gives a strange sound
to some old passages in which they occur, *e.g.* :

> "What remains past cure
> Bear not too *sensibly*",

says Dalila, in *Samson Agonistes*, meaning, 'Be not too sensitive
about what cannot be helped'.

52. **embraced heaviness** = grief which he hugs. It is characteristic of Antonio that he 'gives way' to emotion. For 'embraced'
compare 'rash-embraced despair' in iii. 2. 109.

Scene 9.

*The Prince of Arragon makes his choice among the caskets, and
chooses the silver one.*

While Bassanio is on his way to Belmont, another suitor tries his
fortune. This is a grandee of Spain. He is similar in some respects,
in rank and splendour, to the Prince of Morocco. But his pride is
of another kind altogether from that of the Moor. It is not boyish
vanity, but impracticable self-conceit. A passage in Mr. Strachan-
Davidson's *Cicero* ("Heroes of the Nations" series, pp. 192, 193)
illustrates these two kinds of vanity: "Two faults, of very different
degrees of blackness, are liable to be confused under the common
name of vanity or self-conceit. There are men into whose souls the
poison seems to have eaten deep; they are pompous, overweening,
repellent; their power of judgment and of action is impaired; . . .
Sometimes, on the other hand, vanity is a mere superficial weakness,
the accompaniment of a light heart, a quick, sensitive temperament,
an unsuspicious loquacity, and an innocent love of display. Carlyle
has hit off the difference very happily in the contrast which he draws
between Boswell and his father: 'Old Auchinleck had, if not the
gay tail-spreading peacock vanity of his son, no little of the slow-
stalking contentious hissing vanity of the gander, a still more fatal
species'."

Arragon's vanity is of the 'gander-species'. He does not, like
Morocco, allow himself to be carried away by an impulsive and
generous fancy. He scarcely makes any reference to Portia at all,
and chooses on grounds wholly unconnected with her, or with anything, but a belief in himself. She takes his measure in the biting
phrase,

> "O these deliberate fools! When they do choose
> They have the wisdom by their wit to lose",

and treats him with a scarcely concealed dislike very different from
the courtesy she had shown to the Moor.

3. **presently.** See note on ii. 6. 65.

26. meant by the fool multitude, *i.e.* meant to apply to the fool multitude.

27. fond = foolish. So in iii. 3. 9.

32. jump with = 'be at one with'. Cf. *Richard III.*, iii. 1. 11, (a man's outward show) "seldom or never jumpeth with the heart", and the common proverb, "Great minds jump together".

34. then to thee. What must be supplied here? See note on ii. 2. 100.

41. degrees, steps or grades in distinction. The word in Shakespeare's time was not limited, as it is now, to 'degrees' in university rank. Compare the ballad-phrase 'a squire of low degree'.

42. clear honour, *i.e.* 'honour innocently won'. Similarly 'clear' is applied to allegiance in *Macbeth* in the sense of 'unstained loyalty'. Note that 'clear' is not an ordinary attributive adjective here, but that its meaning is as it were diffused through the whole sentence; "Would that honour were won by merit and so won innocently". See note on iii. 2. 165.

44. cover, *i.e.* keep the hat on, as a sign of superiority of rank. Comp. iii. 5. 31.

53. Too long a pause for that, *i.e.* the pause is so long that what you find there cannot be what you are expecting. Arragon tries to argue against the decision of the 'lottery', instead of accepting it, like Morocco.

61. Means 'You must not wish to be both defendant and judge in your own cause, for the two offices are inconsistent with one another'.

63. I wis. See *wis* in the Glossary.

71. You are sped, your destiny is decided.

84. What would my lord? Portia rebukes, by imitation, the affectedly pompous tone of her gentleman-in-waiting. Mr. Beeching quotes, as parallel, *Richard II.*, v. 5. 67—

> *Groom.* "Hail royal prince".
> *King.* "Thanks, noble peer".

88. sensible regreets, *i.e.* substantial or tangible tokens of respect.

89. commends and courteous breath, greetings and verbal courtesy. For 'courteous breath' compare

> "It must appear in other ways than words,
> Therefore I scant this *breathing courtesy*", v. 1. 141.

92–94. Portia might have forgiven him for the sake of these three beautifully musical lines.

97. high-day wit, the opposite of 'work-a-day words'. So in *Merry Wives of Windsor*, young Fenton is said to 'speak holiday'.

Act III.

In the preceding act the main subject was the elopement of the miser's daughter.

In this it is the choice of the right casket by Bassanio. But, to begin with, we have a scene that shows the consequences of Jessica's flight, and prepares us for Shylock's insistence on his bond.

Scene I.

Of Antonio's losses at sea, and of Shylock's intended revenge.

2. It lives there unchecked, *i.e.* the report remains uncontradicted.

This phrase and what follows show that a long time had elapsed in the interval between the second and third acts. Tubal has had time to go to Genoa and return. The bond is within a fortnight of expiry (line 106).

6. my gossip report. Report is figured as a talkative old woman, fond of ginger, and full of pretended emotions. (For other such 'picture-phrases' in Shakespeare, see i. 2. 17, 18.)

honest of her word, another specimen for a collection of idiomatic uses of this preposition. See also 'slips *of* prolixity' in line 10 below.

8. knapped = not 'snapped', as in 'he knappeth the spear in sunder', but 'gnawed' or 'nibbled'. See Glossary, and Furness' note in his Variorum Edition.

10. the plain highway of talk. Similarly Hamlet calls conventional conversation 'the beaten way of friendship', *Hamlet*, ii. 2, 276.

17. cross my prayer, that is, come between Salanio and Salarino before the former could say his prayer, 'Amen' or 'so be it', to confirm the latter's good wishes.

20. none so well, none so well. Though weeks have passed since Jessica's flight, Shylock's rage is not abated. His own fury, the mockery of his enemies, the jeering of the boys in the streets have driven him to a point not far short of madness; and his passion appears in his convulsive and broken sentences, and the repetition of phrases. He has a 'hunted' look, and seems older, wilder, and more neglectful of himself than in the earlier scenes.

34. rhenish, a 'hock', or white wine, is contrasted with red wine.

36. bankrupt, one whose 'bank' is broken, either

(*a*) referring to the original meaning of 'bank', the bench or wooden stall at which a merchant sat, or

(*b*) referring to the use of 'bank' for capital or stock of money. Compare below, line 97, "he cannot choose but break".

37. a prodigal. This word, as applied to Antonio, has given some trouble to the critics. But Shylock's peculiar habit of regarding money naturally comes out in his use of words, which are, so to say, scaled on a different principle from that of the rest of mankind. Launcelot thought himself starved in the Jew's service, but to Shylock he appeared to be a 'huge feeder', and to 'gormandise'. So Antonio is a 'prodigal', though others would only have called him 'generous' or 'munificent'.

41. let him look to his bond. The phrase is repeated three times with increased feeling, and a peculiar emphasis on the last word.

43. It has been pointed out that Shakespeare is in prose-writing not less great than in verse. The paragraph that follows is a superb instance of his skill in 'oratory', so rhythmical in sound, so keen in argument, so overwhelming in passion. Yet it is so true to the character and the 'situation' that it appears inevitable and necessary, an effect of nature, not of art. On the stage, in the mouth of a great actor, the speech excites the hearers, almost beyond endurance, to pity and terror. Even Salanio and Salarino have no answer to it.

58. sufferance, endurance or patience, as in i. 3. 100.

60. it shall go hard but, &c., *i.e.* if I fail to improve upon my pattern it will not be for want of endeavour.

62. Antonio *sends for* his friends. His troubles have depressed him, and he avoids coming out of doors. The intimacy of Antonio with those who had helped in Jessica's elopement, expressed in such a message as this, still further inflames Shylock's anger.

71. For the omission of the relative, see note on i. 1. 175.

72. The curse seems to refer to some such place in the Bible as that in *Daniel,* ix. 11: "All Israel have transgressed thy law; . . . therefore *the curse* is poured upon us, and the oath that is written in the law of Moses". This again refers back to the terrible curse denounced against Israel, if it should not keep the Law, in *Deuteronomy,* xxviii. 15–68, many of the points of which would apply to Shylock's state, *e.g.* "Thy daughters shall be given unto another people, and thine eyes shall look and fail with longing for them all the day long. All thy labours shall a nation which thou knowest not eat up; and thou shalt be only oppressed and crushed alway".

75. would my daughter were dead. Such 'wild and whirling words' must not in fairness be pressed further against Shylock than similar speeches against Lear. And in any case they are not merely the utterance of disappointed avarice. Jessica was already 'dead' to him and to his nation in Shylock's belief; she had 'cut herself off' from her people.

77. Why, so. Shylock mutters as he makes rough calculation of the different sums lost.

102. Out upon her! The expression 'out upon' seems an extension of such a phrase as that found in the *Lucrece,*

"*Out*, idle words! servants to shallow fools".

103. Leah. The touch comes unexpectedly, and carries the mind of the hearer back to other days in Shylock's life with a bitterness of contrast hardly less sharp than in the terrible place in *Macbeth*, ii. 2. 14.

110. at our synagogue. Places of worship were common resorts for business in Shakespeare's day (*e.g.* St. Paul's, in London). So that it is perhaps fanciful to press the reference here as François Victor Hugo does in a passage quoted by Furness: "The Jew invokes the Ancient of Days who spoke unto Moses aforetime: 'If a man cause a blemish in his neighbour, as he hath done, so shall it be done to him; breach for breach, eye for eye, tooth for tooth'. In entering his synagogue, Shylock entrusts his hatred to the safeguard of his Faith". Yet it is certainly true that Shylock regards himself as 'the depositary of the vengeance of his race' and religion. (Compare, at the trial, "I have an oath in heaven", and above, on hearing of Antonio's losses, "I thank God, I thank God". See also iv. 1. 36.)

Scene 2.

How Bassanio, by discerning truth from show, makes choice of the right casket, and so achieves his quest; how news arrives from Venice that Antonio has lost all his ships and is in prison for Bassanio's sake; how Portia speeds Bassanio on his way to save his friend.

This is the middle point of the action where the intricacy of the plot is at its greatest. In the course of this scene the three stories become one, the issue of which Portia takes upon herself.

An interval of more than a fortnight has elapsed since the last scene. The bond is forfeit, and a messenger will, ere the scene be over, have had time to arrive from Venice to report Antonio's danger.

"Enter Bassanio, Portia, &c., *and Attendants.*" They must woo, like sovereign princes, each at the head of a retinue. How nobly and gracefully it is done!

6. quality. See Glossary for different uses of this word in the play.

15. o'erlook'd. To 'overlook' was to cast a spell upon, by means of the 'glamour' or power of the eye. So it comes to have the meaning of 'to blight' with the evil eye, as in *Merry Wives*, v. 5. 87:

"Vile worm, thou wast o'erlook'd even in thy birth".

20. The line must be read:

"And so', | though yo' | urs, not' | yours, prove' | it so'".

'Yours' is dissyllabic at first, then monosyllabic, after the strongly accented 'not'. Compare the line in the *Tempest*:

"Twelve ye' | är since', | Miran' | da, twelve' | year since'".

See Abbott, *Shakesp. Grammar*, § 475 and § 480.

22, 23. peize and **eke.** 'peize' means to keep suspended, 'eke' to make longer; together they mean 'to delay'.

29. fear the enjoying, *i.e.* 'fear that I shall not enjoy'; as in v. 1. 273, 'fear keeping safe' means 'fear that I may not keep safe'.

33. Torture was applied in Great Britain to a prisoner suspected of treason as late as 1690. The opinion that Portia utters here of its uselessness became established by the beginning of the eighteenth century. It was never sanctioned by English 'Common Law', but inflicted by ministers of the crown with sovereign authority. "The rack seldom stood idle in the Tower for all the latter part of Elizabeth's reign" (Hallam, *Const. Hist.*, vol. i.).

39. Verb of motion omitted, as in ii. 2. 100, &c.

41. True love will give the necessary insight. Compare i. 2. 27.

44. The legend of the swan's death-song is found in Greek literature. Tennyson has given a poem to it, 'The Dying Swan', and a fine simile in the *Passing of Arthur*:

> "the barge with oar and sail
> Moved from the brink, like some full-breasted swan
> That, *fluting a wild carol ere her death*,
> Ruffles her pure cold plume, and takes the flood
> With swarthy webs".

55. young Alcides. The story of the rescue of Hesione, daughter of Laomedon, by Hercules, is told by Ovid, *Metam.* xi. 199 f. The love of Hercules is here said to have been not so great as that of Bassanio, because he saved Hesione for the sake of certain horses which Laomedon offered him. He gave Hesione to Telamon. All the detail of this picture is Shakespeare's.

56. howling Troy, *i.e.* loudly lamenting. So in the Authorized Version of *Isaiah*, xxiii. 6, "howl, ye inhabitants of the isle".
In the splendid series of images with which this speech is filled, Portia shows how deeply her heart and imagination are touched.

Song. What is the metre of the song?

63. fancy, that is, love, in which sense the word is common in Elizabethan English, *e.g.*—

> "In maiden meditation, fancy-free",

a line in which the last two words are often misquoted and misunderstood.

73. So may the outward shows. The "so" does not refer to anything in the song, but to some previous thought of the speaker's. We only hear the conclusion of Bassanio's comments.

least themselves, *i.e.* least like the reality within.

74. still = always.

82. his, where we should expect 'its'. See Abbott, *Shakes. Gr.*, § 228, where it is shown that 'its' was a new word, only formed in Shakespeare's lifetime, and scarcely used by him except in his later plays.

84. **stairs of sand.** The phrase is a curious but most expressive one. Nothing could be imagined more untrustworthy than a stair of sand. There is therefore no need to press the spelling of the early editions—'stayers' or 'staiers',—and to suppose that the word means 'props', as Knight suggested.

85. **beards,** used for hair on the face generally, and sometimes for 'moustache' or 'whiskers', particularly the military moustache, *e.g.* in the famous phrase which Jaques uses of the soldier, "*bearded* like a pard".

86. **white livers.** See note on ii. 1. 7.

87. **excrement.** Cf. *Love's Labour's Lost*, v. 1. 109: "Dally with my excrement, with my mustachio". See Glossary.

88. **beauty.** There are many references in Shakespeare to the practice of 'making up' complexions, *e.g. Hamlet*, iii. 1. 51, a cheek "*beautied* with plastering art"; and 149, "I have heard of your paintings, too; God has given you one face and you make yourselves another".

91. **lightest,** *i.e.* fickle, 'light o' love'.

92. **golden locks.** Bassanio is so absorbed in his reflections that he seems to have forgotten the colour of his own lady's hair. See i. 1. 169, 170.

94. **supposed fairness,** false beauty; 'known' does not qualify 'fairness' but 'locks'.

96. **The skull that bred them in the sepulchre.** What word might be inserted after 'them' to make the construction plainer? What is such a construction called?

97. **guiled shore.** See Glossary.

99. **an Indian beauty.** If the text be right, the last word is used ironically in contrast with the direct sense of 'beauteous' in the previous line. But the repetition of the word suggests a printer's error, and it is possible that we have not got the passage as Shakespeare wrote it. It has been proposed to alter the punctuation, and to put a semicolon after 'Indian'. (See Appendix on the Text.)

100. **times.** The word offers a pretty exercise in interpretation. What does Shakespeare signify by it? and what similar uses can you quote? (You will find one in *Timon of Athens*, iv. 3. 519—

"Doubt and suspect, alas, are placed too late:
You should have feared *false times* when you did feast".)

102. **hard food for Midas:** a whole story in a phrase. The tale is told by Ovid, in the eleventh book of the *Metamorphoses*. The student should collect for himself all the passages in this play which contain references to classical stories. Shakespeare realized these stories so vividly that he could say what occurred between one

incident and another, where the classical story-teller himself had not filled the gap. *e.g.* in the wonderful simile:

> " Even such a man, so faint, so spiritless,
> So dull, so dead in look, so woe-begone,
> Drew Priam's curtain in the dead of night,
> And would have told him half his Troy was burnt,
> But Priam found the fire, ere he his tongue ".
>
> —*2 Henry IV.*, i. 1. 70.

103. pale and common drudge. It is curious that the ' paleness ' of silver repels Bassanio, whilst that of lead moves him ' more than eloquence '. Taking the words as they stand, we must be careful to emphasize '*thy*' at the beginning of line 106, and suppose a contrast between the paleness of the public slave and that of the stern challenger. But here also, as in 99, the repetition of the word suggests a printer's error. Warburton's emendation of ' paleness ' to ' plainness ' seems likely to be right.

109. thoughts, anxieties, as in the common Elizabethan phrase, ' to take thought ', *i.e.* to brood over cares.

124. having made one. Analyse the whole sentence. In what respect does it differ from the usual grammatical forms?

131. continent. Shakespeare, in spite of his ' small Latin ', uses derivatives from that language with a clear feeling for their original senses. As he gives to ' continent ' the meaning of ' that which holds ', so in *Hamlet*, to ' extravagant and erring ', that of ' roaming and straying '.

140. Notice the effect produced here, as in line 110 and the following, by the rhymed passage. The speech of the lovers grows musical with happiness.

142. contending in a prize, that is, in a race for a prize.

158. livings, properties.

159. account, sum, in gross. The metaphors are drawn from a merchant's books. With noble courage and grace Portia speaks openly of that which any woman less sincere or less wise would have tried to pass over or to disparage—her wealth, wishes it sixty times as great as it is, then by one gift abolishes it, and presents herself to Bassanio, as she is, by herself alone. The simplicity and humanity of the words here are more ' symptomatic ' of the real nature of Portia than the oratory in the trial scene.

163, 164. can learn, '*may* learn'. The original distinction in meaning between ' can ' and ' may ' is here maintained. To ' can ' is to know, to have the wit or skill to do something. To ' may ' is to have the thing in one's might or power. Thus ' may ' here means I am not disabled by age; ' can ' means further, I have the faculty to learn.

165. her gentle spirit commits itself, is equivalent to ' her spirit gently commits itself '. The force of the adjective is diffused over the whole phrase. Compare the expression in *Macbeth*, i. 6. : "the air Nimbly and sweetly recommends itself Unto our gentle senses": or in this play, iii. 4. 36, where 'fair' similarly seems to qualify more than the substantive to which it is attached.

169, 171. But now . . . but now, expresses complete and sudden change from one moment to another.

179. The excited feelings are compared here to a crowd of loyal subjects in a state of joyous uproar, as in *Julius Cæsar* they are compared to subjects in insurrection:

> "The genius and the mortal instruments
> Are then in council, and the state of man—
> Like to a little kingdom—suffers then
> The nature of an insurrection".

183. Each cry is a 'something', a word with a meaning, but when all are mixed together they become inarticulate, 'a wild of nothing', a chaos without meaning; and yet not without meaning, for the very noise is expressive of delight. Schlegel's translation is an admirable commentary on this passage:

> "Wo jedes Etwas in einander flieszend,
> Zu einem Chaos wird von nichts als Freude,
> Laut und doch sprachlos".

193. from me. There is a play here on the double meaning of the preposition, either "given by" or "taken from". Taken in the second sense, the phrase means, as Johnson points out, "none away from me, none that I shall lose if you gain it". The quibble is slight enough, but any quip is worth making to relieve the solemn insipidity of a formal congratulation. Here again Schlegel is the best commentary:

> "Ich wünsch' euch was für Freud' ihr wünschen könnt
> Denn sicher wünscht ihr keine von mir weg".

For a very similar quibble on two senses of 'from', compare *Richard III.*, iv. 4. 255-260.

195. bargain, that is, contract. The word is, of course, used without any implication of gain to one party as compared with the other. It is interesting to collect from the play all the instances of words which have modified their meaning since Shakespeare's time, such as 'complexion', 'estate', 'shrewd', 'convenient', 'envy', &c.

197. so=provided that.

216. Salanio, spelt very variously in the early editions. The Cambridge editors understand a new personage to be introduced here, called 'Salerio'. I prefer to follow Dyce and Furness and Beeching, and to regard the variations as printer's errors. In the previous scene Antonio had sent for Salanio and Salarino. One of them remained in Venice to comfort the Merchant, the other sped to Belmont to procure rescue.

225. Lorenzo excuses himself for his appearance without invitation. Salanio had pressed him to come, with a "reason for it". He wished to summon all Antonio's friends into council.

233. estate, condition, where we should rather use the other 'doublet' *state*. Compare the gradual differentiation of 'history' and 'story', 'to' and 'too', 'of' and 'off'. In line 256 below, contrariwise, 'state' is used where we should say 'estate'. By this ambiguous answer we are meant to understand that Antonio was afflicted not in mind or body, but in estate.

236. royal merchant, not in any technical sense of 'privileged', as some of the commentators suppose, but 'princely', 'munificent', as Antony calls Cæsar 'royal and loving'.

239. We are the Jasons. The story of the *Life and Death of Jason* should, by any who are not familiar with it, be read in William Morris' poem. This line contains a clear reminiscence of one in Marlowe's *The Jew of Malta* (in rhythm as well as in meaning): "I'll be thy Jason, thou my golden fleece" (Act iv. sc. 4).

240. shrewd, spiteful, bad, means literally 'accursed'.

245. I am half yourself. Compare what Brutus' Portia says to him (*Julius Cæsar*, ii. 1. 267):

> "No, my Brutus;
> You have some sick offence within your mind
> Which by the right and virtue of my place
> I ought to know of; . . .
> . . unfold to me, *your self, your half,*
> Why you are heavy".

259. his mere enemy. *Mere*, by derivation, means unmixed, pure. In modern usages, *e.g.* a 'mere trifle', it has a depreciatory sense, 'nothing more than'. In this passage it signifies 'thorough-going', 'intense'.

273. confound = overthrow, as in the "let me never be confounded" of the *Te Deum* in the Book of Common Prayer.

275. impeach the freedom, *i.e.* he threatens an action to annul the city's charter. Shakespeare uses terms that would be vividly understood by English citizens possessed of rights to administer justice by royal charter. Compare iv. 1. 39, where Shylock says:

> "If you deny it, let the danger light
> Upon your charter and your city's freedom".

Venice, of course, was not a 'free city' in the sense that her judicial powers depended on a charter; she was an independent sovereign state. In such points as this Shakespeare used the terms of his own country and his own time, as being to his hearers the truest and most vivid; just as the 'Old Masters' painted the persons of Hebrew history in the dress of their own Italian countrymen; or as the German schoolboy, quoted by Jespersen (*Progress in Lan-*

guage, p. 363), described Hannibal as swearing to be always a *Frenchman* towards the Romans.

Ruskin, in an interesting place, extracted in the *Frondes Agrestes*, defends the Shakespearean practice as being right and true, in contrast to modern 'realism'.

279. envious=hateful, as 'envy'=hatred, in iv. 1. 126.

282. Chus, *i.e.* Cush, a name taken, like Tubal, from one of the early chapters of Genesis.

Jessica's recollections here make it certain that an interval of some length of time must be supposed to elapse between the events in Act i. and those in Act ii.

290. That is, 'the best-condition'd and *most* unwearied spirit', the superlative in 'best' is carried on to 'unwearied'. Refer back to note on ii. 1. 46.

308. you shall hence, verb of motion implied, as in ii. 2. 100.

311. Since you are dear-bought, I will love you dear. Portia has a delightful way of relieving from embarrassment those on whom she bestows kindness. Here she covers her generosity under what seems a rather spiteful pun, and so escapes, and gives escape to her friends. For a similar instance of her 'tact', see v. 1. 137.

So rapidly and brilliantly does she rise to the occasion here that she hardly gives us time to realize the sacrifice she is making. It is all the more heroic that she spares us the 'heroics'. By an effort of clear imagination, she sees that Bassanio would never afterwards have forgiven himself if he had hesitated now. By prompt self-suppression she makes it easy for him to do the right thing.

315. between you and I. Jespersen, *Progress in Language*, p. 246, says, " *I* was preferred to *me* after *and* because the group of words 'you and I' would occur in everyday speech so frequently as to make it practically a sort of stock-phrase taken as a whole, the last word of which was therefore not inflected". He quotes a number of instances similar to this from great writers, to which we may add that 'Mr. Perker' uses this very phrase in chapter x. of the *Pickwick Papers*.

Scene 3.

The three months having expired, and the bond being forfeit, Antonio has been cast into prison; guarded by a gaoler, he now seeks an interview with Shylock, who refuses to hear him.

A short interval of time has elapsed since the last scene. The trial is fixed for the morrow. Antonio is expecting the arrival of Bassanio.

9. naughty, fond, have altered in sense somewhat since Shakespeare's time. 'Naughty' was not then confined to children, nor used in a half-humorous way, but meant as much as 'wicked', 'worthless'. Compare v. 1. 91 :

> " So shines a good deed in a *naughty* world".

What is the derivation of the word?
For 'fond', see Glossary.

18. impenetrable, whose heart cannot be touched. We may compare Cloten's use of 'penetrate' in *Cymbeline*, ii. 3. 14: "I am advised to give her music o' mornings; they say it will *penetrate*".

19. kept, lived. To 'keep' remains in this sense among Cambridge undergraduates.

27. The reading followed here is Theobald's. See Appendix on the Text.

Scene 4.

How Portia, leaving the charge of her house to Lorenzo and Jessica, departs, under pretence of a vow, for Venice, to aid her husband in the rescue of Antonio.

The time is the afternoon of the day on which Bassanio made his choice among the caskets. After a hasty ceremony of marriage, he has parted from his wife at the door of the church. She and the rest of the company have just returned to the house. (From v. 1. 249, it appears that Portia left Belmont almost immediately after Bassanio.) Full of the daring plan she has devised, she astonishes Lorenzo by the courage she shows at her lord's departure.

2. conceit is by derivation the same word as 'concept', from which it has become 'differentiated' gradually, both in spelling and in sense (compare 'estate' and 'state', 'history' and 'story'). In meaning, 'conceit' has passed from a notion or idea in general to a quaint or fanciful notion, and finally to a notion of one's own importance. Here it still bears its original meaning of idea or conception. Compare i. 1. 92.

3. godlike amity. Lorenzo means that Portia shows her esteem of friendship as something higher than human by speeding Bassanio on his way at such a moment. There is not a *conflict* here, as has been sometimes said, between love and friendship. It is more correct to say that Portia feels the truth of her husband's love involved in the loyalty of his friendship; but indeed Shakespeare in this scene, as often elsewhere, uses the same word 'love' of both passions, as the cavalier did of devotion to his mistress and devotion to his cause :

> "I could not love thee, dear, so much,
> Loved I not honour more".

9. = Than commonplace kindness can oblige you to be.

11. For the double negative, compare iv. 1. 56, 73, 159.

12. waste the time, spend the time (just as Valentine says in *Two Gentlemen of Verona*, ii. 4. 63, "We have conversed and spent our hours together"). 'Waste' has here no sense of unprofitableness. Rolfe compares Milton (Sonnet to Mr. Lawrence),

"Help waste a sullen day".

See note on 'bargain', line 195 above, and 'imposition', line 33 below.

15. manners, compare note on ii. 3. 17.

25. husbandry and manage, stewardship and control. What is the derivation of 'husbandry'? To what Greek word, with a common English derivative, does it exactly correspond?

27. I have toward Heaven breathed a secret vow. This vow is not a mere pretext to cover her journey. It is doubly characteristic of Portia, first because such a vow is in keeping with the many small touches by which we learn to think of her as contemplative and devout (*e.g.* i. 2. 11–18, 48, 91, 113; iii. 2. 13; iv. 1. 178–196; v. 1. 89–91); and secondly, because though the vow is in the literal sense set aside or postponed, this only arises from the fact that her noble and brave spirit sees that here she can act as well as pray. Afterwards, when with wit and courage she has done all that was to be done, she fulfils her vow. As she returns home

"She doth stray about
By holy crosses, where she kneels and prays
For happy wedlock hours" (v. 1. 31, 32).

The *vow* is in the spirit of Imogen or Desdemona; the *action* is like Rosalind or Beatrice. The union of the two belongs to Portia.

33. imposition, something 'put upon' a person, but without any of the secondary idea of fraud, which the word often carries in modern English. Compare i. 2. 114.

Another instance of Portia's generosity of mind; she represents her hospitality and trust as a *task* laid upon Lorenzo, and so tries to relieve him from a sense of obligation.

36. in all fair commands, the adjective colours the whole phrase, not 'commands' only. See note on iii. 2. 165.

45. Now, Balthasar. The incident of Balthasar's ride from Belmont to Padua, and from Padua to the Ferry, is one of the most exciting in the play, though it is only by slight touches here and there that we are enabled to follow it.

Bassanio had only been gone an hour or two before the solution occurred to Portia (v. i. 249). She must go herself to Venice. But she wants a lawyer's robes and some notes on technical points of legal procedure. How to get them? There is her kinsman Dr. Bellario of Padua, the most famous jurisconsult in Italy. Her trusty man, Balthasar, must ride on the spur to Padua with a letter to the doctor. Arrived at Padua he finds the lawyer laid up with sickness, but also pen in hand, answering an invitation from the Doge of Venice to come and decide the very case on which Portia had written to him. Cannot the two messages be made to work together? Portia shall be Bellario's deputy to the Doge. While the robes are being fetched, the doctor writes two letters, one, afterwards read aloud in court, to His Grace the Doge, recommending Portia as substitute for himself, under the name Balthasar, borrowed from her messenger; the other to Portia.

Armed with these letters and the precious robes, Balthasar gallops off again to ride through the night, so that he may catch his Lady at the Ferry in the morning. There was no time to be lost, for even Bassanio, travelling straight, would only arrive on the evening before the trial (iii. 3. 34), and he had some hours' start. Balthasar reaches the Ferry in time to meet the lumbering coach which had brought Portia along one side of the triangle, while he had been riding the other two. Portia just reaches the court at the critical instant.

52. imagined speed. Cf. *Sonnet* xliv.—

> " For nimble thought can jump both sea and land
> As soon as think the place where he would be ".

53. traject, Rowe's correction for the printer's error ' tranect'. Hunter quotes from Coryat's *Crudities*, "There are in Venice thirteen ferries or passages, which they commonly call Traghetti ".

56. convenient speed, the speed that suits the occasion.

67. reed voice, ' voix flutée', as F. Victor Hugo translates it.

69. quaint lies, ingenious lies.

72. I could not do withal, ' I could not help it'. Dyce quotes from *Lesclaircissement de la Langue Françoise* (1530), "I can nat do withall, a thyng lyeth nat in me, or I am nat in faulte that a thyng is done ".

77. Jacks, fellows, a term of contempt common in Shakespeare.

80. in my coach, which stays for us At the park gate. Portia throughout this scene shows not only infinite spirit and courage, but a power of combination and decisive command equal to that of Lady Macbeth herself. Compare the words to Balthasar—

> " Waste no time in words,
> But get thee gone : I shall be there before thee ".

Scene 5.

Of Jessica, Lorenzo, and Launcelot at Belmont, and what Jessica says in praise of Portia.

This scene occurs probably just after the departure of Portia and Nerissa.

1. the sins of the father, &c., another instance to be added to a collection of references to the Bible in this play.

2. **I fear you** = I fear for you; compare the note on iii. 2. 29 above, and Abbott, *Shak. Gram.*, § 200.

4. **agitation**, a 'malapropism' for 'cogitation'.

9. **one by another**, means either 'one in competition with another', or 'taking one with another, reckoning all up'.

29. **cover**, a play on two different senses of the word. (i) To put the dishes on the table; (ii) to put the hat on the head.

32. **quarrelling with occasion**, like 'defying the matter' in line 46 below, seems to mean to slight the business in hand for the sake of a verbal quibble.

40. **O dear discretion!** Discretion is invoked as the quality which Launcelot had shown least of. His words are an army, 'suited', that is, in uniform. They correspond to one another, but not to the subject of discourse; they obey his orders like so many soldiers, but he orders them to the wrong posts.

43. **A many.** It is one of the curiosities of language that we still say 'a few', while 'a many' has become obsolete, or only provincial. The phrase is to be explained as a 'collective'.

44. **Garnish'd like him.** Does this mean as ill-furnished with discretion as Launcelot? The habit of quibbling and punning was universal in Shakespeare's time. Compare note on i. 2. 7.

52. **merit it**, Pope's emendation. The double 'it' at the end of the line seems to have led to misprints.

62. **stomach** = appetite.

Act IV.—Scene I.

Of the trial of the cause between Shylock the Jew and Antonio the merchant; how Portia, disguised as a Doctor of Civil Law, delivers Antonio out of the hand of Shylock; and how Bassanio is persuaded to give the Doctor his betrothal ring, which he had vowed never to part from but with his life.

The scene which follows answers in some points to the scene of Bassanio's choice of the leaden casket. To the eye it is even more splendid; the background is the great hall of the High Court of Justice; in front is a throng of eager people, Antonio's merchant-friends from the Rialto, Bassanio's companions-in-arms, and magnificoes from the ducal court, all in dress of many colours; round the bench and near the prisoner stand ruffed halberdiers; aloft sits the Doge, in crimson velvet with an upper garment 'of white cloth of silver, with great massy buttons of gold'; a degree below him sit the Senators in red cloth tipped with white ermine; on the right, in earnest talk with Bassanio and Gratiano, stands Antonio, ready for either issue; and, presently, on the left, enter, with bond and knife and scales, Shylock, alone.

1. What, where we should rather say 'now', or 'well'. Compare, "What, Jessica", ii. 5. 3 and 4.

5. Uncapable. It has been pointed out that the use of 'un-' and 'in-' in compounds varies capriciously, or by laws of euphony so delicate that they cannot be analysed. Thus we say, '*un*equal' but '*in*equality', '*un*grateful' but '*in*gratitude'.

5, 6. empty from is equal to 'empty of'. This double use is like the Latin construction with genitive or ablative in the case of a word such as *egeo*.

7. qualify, *i.e.* to temper, or alter by mixing or blending. The word carries on the metaphor implied in 'dram of mercy'.

10. envy. See Glossary on the word.

16. Make room, indicates the crowded state of the court.

18. *i.e.* 'that you are carrying this show of hatred up to the moment when you would have to carry it into action'.

20. remorse. See Glossary.

29. royal merchant. Here the phrase seems to have the technical meaning which it has not in iii. 2. 236. It signifies a merchant of such wealth and position as to be dignified with a special title from the court.

39. charter and freedom. See note on iii. 2. 276.

43. it is my humour. The word contains a reference to the strange physiological theories of the Middle Ages, whereby certain mental dispositions were connected with different 'moistures' or 'humours' of the body. Many terms still in use are derived from this old belief, such as 'phlegm' and 'phlegmatic' applied to temper; 'choleric', 'melancholy', 'sanguine', &c. The 'temperament' or 'complexion' of a man was thought to depend on the blend of his humours.

43, and following. These lines contain Shylock's first defence for his insistence on the execution of his bond. Some feelings, he says, are ultimate; they cannot be further analysed. They resemble hysterical states, or strange bodily impulses over which the reason has no control, such as, instinctive fear of certain animals. Of this sort is my antipathy to Antonio.

47. gaping pig. Malone quotes from Nashe's *Pierce Penilesse*: "Some will take on like a mad man if they see a pigge come to the table". A boar's head was, and is, served with a lemon in its open mouth.

49. for affection, Mistress of passion. Affection here has its old sense of an impulse of any kind. It is distinguished from passion as excitement from feeling, the nervous impulse from the mental state. The whole passage may be rendered, 'For impulse controls feeling, and excites a mood corresponding to itself'. This mood may or may not be *reasonable*. For instance, a cat may cause in some particular individual a nervous shock of the kind which is always connected with the mental feeling of fear. In that case fear will be felt in spite of any reassurance by the reason that the cat cannot do any real harm.

The passage is interesting, both for the subtlety of the argument underlying the simple illustrations quoted by Shylock, and also because it is one where 'emendation' (see Appendix on the Text) has certainly given us Shakespeare's original words. The quartos and folios put a full stop at 'affection', and put 'Masters' or 'Maisters' at the beginning of the next line. The emendation, adopted in the text, is Thirlby's. Dr. Abbott has confirmed it by reference to two other places where 'mastres', 'maistresse', 'mistress', have been confused, viz. *Tempest*, ii. 1. 5; and Beaumont and Fletcher, *The Coxcomb*, ii. 3. 9: "Where be thy mastres, man? I would speak with her".

54. a harmless necessary cat. The phrase is one of those which, for some subtle reason, stick in people's memory, and enter into the language so fully as to be used constantly by folks who could not say where they come from. It is only requisite to look at attempted translations to see that the magic of such phrases is not transferable; *e.g.*

"Un chat, familier et inoffensif" (F. Victor Hugo).

"Katz', ein harmlos nützlich Thier" (Schlegel).

How many of such phrases, since become 'household words', can you collect from this play?

55. a woollen bag-pipe. The adjective refers strictly to the *covering* of the wind-bag. The wind-bag itself is commonly made of 'greased leather', but it is often covered with woollen cloth. It is hard to see why the commentators have made so much difficulty over the epithet, which conveys just the idea of bleating inoffensiveness that the passage requires.

57. lodged hate, *i.e.* hate that has gathered and accumulated.

59. a losing suit, *i.e.* a suit by which he will forego the repayment of his money, and take flesh instead.

61. the current of thy cruelty, a sweeping tide of feeling, just as Othello compares his own wrath

"to the Pontic sea,
Whose icy *current* and compulsive course
Ne'er feels retiring ebb".

62, and following. Mark the peculiarly forcible effect of the thrust and counter-thrust of the argument in these epigrammatic single lines.

63. Bassanio's question contains the refutation of Shylock's philosophy. 'True, we *have* feelings, produced by external physical causes, feelings which we cannot keep from arising. But we need not *act* upon them, unless we will to do it.'

67. think you question = remember you are holding converse with.

73. no noise with 'forbid' makes a double negative, as in 56 above and 157 below.

74. fretten. See Abbott, § 344.

79. conveniency, promptitude or despatch.

86. What judgment shall I dread, doing no wrong? This is Shylock's second defence. He here takes 'wrong' to mean that which is contrary to statute law, and denies therefore that he himself is doing any wrong. He thus occupies the position of the Scribes and Pharisees of the time of Christ, when, for instance, they considered it no 'wrong' to refuse help to near relatives, so long as the formula of the Law respecting 'Corban' was properly observed. He claims the literal fulfilment of legal obligations, and believes 'right' to consist in that. See, further, note on line 200.

88. Shylock's third line of argument : 'You admit property in human flesh by allowing the purchase of slaves. I have acquired property in a pound of Antonio's flesh. Grant me possession of that which is lawfully mine.'

The argument here is far stronger than that in Silvayn's *Orator*, with which it has been compared. Silvayn's Jew claims to be allowed to take a pound of flesh as a *milder penalty* for a defaulting debtor than the common one of slavery. Shylock bases his claim on the *same principle* as that implied in the purchase of slaves. The court, as is evident from line 101, feel the argument unanswerable.

89. parts, functions, duties.

101. Upon my power, by my constitutional authority.

Up to this point Shylock has had the advantage over his enemies, and despair settles upon Antonio's friends. There seems no alternative but either to grant the Jew his forfeit or to adjourn the court. It is now that the Duke mentions that he has sent for Bellario, and it is now that we hear of Portia's arrival in Venice, only just in time for her purpose.

111. A tainted wether, touched with some disease or disabled by some accident. For the bearing of this passage on the character of Antonio, see the study in the Introduction.

120. Not on thy sole, but on thy soul. In Shakespeare's time these two words were not, as now, pronounced exactly alike, but 'soul' was longer, almost dissyllabic in sound. The same play on words occurs in Act i. sc. 1 of *Julius Cæsar.* This passage between Shylock and Gratiano takes place while the Duke reads Bellario's letter.

122. hangman's axe, hangman was used in quite a general sense as an 'executioner', whatever the method of execution might be.

123. envy. See Glossary on the word.

125. inexorable is the correction of the Third Folio for the earlier 'inexecrable'. Dr. Abbott attempts to defend the latter, as meaning 'not to be execrated enough', 'too bad for execration', which does not fit in with the first half of the line; while, on the other hand, 'inexorable' just carries on the sense of the end of line 123.

126 seems to mean 'Let justice be blamed for having allowed you to live so long'.

128. To hold, *i.e.* so as to hold. Pythagoras and his doctrine of the transmigration of souls are referred to also in *Twelfth Night* and *As You Like It*, two plays written perhaps not much later than the *Merchant of Venice*.

131. a wolf, hang'd for human slaughter. "On the Continent, down to a comparatively late period, the lower animals were in all respects considered amenable to the laws. Domestic animals were tried in the common criminal courts, and their punishment on conviction was death; wild animals fell under the jurisdiction of the ecclesiastical courts." Trials of domestic animals were founded "on the Jewish Law, as laid down in *Exodus*, xxi. 28". The last trial and execution of an animal (a cow) in France took place in 1740. See the amusing article in Chambers' *Book of Days*, vol. i. pp. 126–8.

132. The belief in the interchange of souls between men and wolves is ancient and wide-spread, and has led to some of the most uncanny stories in existence. See Baring Gould's *Book of the Werewolf*; and, for the connection of the belief with that in the transmigration of souls, see Tylor's *Anthropology*.

157. impediment to let him lack, is to be compared with 'forbid to make no noise', above, line 73. There is a negative too many for modern English grammar in these constructions, though not for good Elizabethan, any more than for good Greek. Compare 'just cause or impediment why these two persons should not be joined together', where the positive word 'cause' is coupled with the negative 'impediment'.

163. Enter Portia.

Up to now, as Booth, the great American actor, notes (quoted by Furness), Shylock has fixed all his attention upon the Duke, and has shown only contempt for the other persons present. Bellario's letter disturbs him, and he anxiously watches the young lawyer as he comes into court.

Observe that Portia comes, as Bellario's deputy, to 'determine' the cause (line 103 above). She is therefore judge, not advocate. She takes command of the whole cause, and speaks with the authority of the whole court (line 294 below).

For a similar case, in Spanish law, of the delegation of a judicial decision to a 'referee' in the person of a jurisconsult, see an extremely

interesting note by J. T. Doyle, quoted on page 417 of Furness'
Variorum Edition.

164. Take your place, that is, on the judge's bench. The Duke
has been so perplexed by the subtlety and vigour with which Shylock
has put his case that he is glad enough to leave the responsibility
of deciding to someone else. Portia could not have had so free a
hand if she had arrived earlier.

172, 173. 'Yet in such a form that no technical objection can be
raised to your procedure.'

174. danger is an ancient legal term, derived from Low Latin
dominium, and meaning (i) absolute control in general, (ii) the
special form of control conferred by the allowance of a legal claim.
The words may be rendered, 'You come under his claim, do you
not?'

176. Then must the Jew be merciful, *i.e.* the Jew *must* be
merciful, if the case is to end well. Shylock takes the word in its
legal sense.

178. 'Mercy is a virtue that is not to be forced'; "la clémence ne
se commande pas", as F. Victor Hugo translates it. For 'quality'
see Glossary. **strained** = forced or constrained.

185. attribute to awe, that which properly belongs to awe, its
characteristic symbol. In line 189 below, 'attribute' signifies 'property' or 'natural quality'.

194. We do pray for mercy, refers, of course, to a clause in the
Lord's Prayer, which Portia takes for granted that Shylock knows.

200. My deeds upon my head! Shakespeare may have had in
his mind a similar cry in a court of justice, "His blood be upon us
and upon our children" (*Matt.*, xxvii. 25).

I crave the Law! or as he said before, "I stand here for Law!"
This claim of Shylock's, with the appeal of Portia to which it is a
reply, may be paralleled with many passages in the Epistles of Saint
Paul, where the demand of the strict Jew for the literal fulfilment of
the whole of the Law is shown to be self-destructive and to lead of
necessity to an Equity or Charity which transcends, but does not
evade it. (See particularly Epistle to the Galatians, chaps. ii., iii.,
and iv.) This Equity is not to be Lawlessness, but a newer and
more perfect Law.

In this as in other points Shakespeare intended Shylock to embody
the Jewish spirit as he conceived it. Similarly Portia's position is
not less clearly thought out nor less subtly maintained, as we shall
see when we reach its final development. But, once more, we must
be on our guard against supposing that Shakespeare's chief object
was to illustrate two opposing philosophical views. His purpose was
to portray Shylock and Portia truthfully. (See Appendix 'On the
Meaning of the Play'.)

212. It must not be. Portia's refusal to 'wrest the law' here reminds us of her saying in i. 2. 92, "If I live to be as old as Sibylla, I will die as chaste as Diana, unless I be obtained by the manner of my father's will". Compare also iii. 2. 12.

217. A Daniel come to judgement! refers to a story in the Apocrypha, in which Daniel is narrated to have delivered, by his shrewdness, a woman suffering under false accusation.

219. Let me look upon the bond. Portia goes concisely, but gradually to her point. She wishes (i) to give full opportunity to both sides to 'say their say', (ii) to prove to the uttermost that Shylock's aim was, not the recovery of his losses, but the 'judicial murder' of Antonio.

241–243, *i.e.* the scope of the law certainly includes the exaction of a forfeit, whatever that forfeit may be. In this case there is no doubt that the forfeit is clearly described in the bond.

245. more elder. Double signs for the comparative and superlative degrees of adjectives are common in Shakespeare, *e.g.*:

> " This was the most unkindest cut of all "
> (*Julius Cæsar*, iii. 2. 187).

249. Are there balance? See Abbott, § 471. The plural and possessive of nouns in which the singular ends in a sibilant, such as 's', 'se', 'ce', &c., are frequently written without the additional syllable, *e.g. Sonnet* cxii.:

> " my adder's *sense*
> To critic and to flatterer stoppèd *are*".

258. I am arm'd, *i.e.* 'with a quietness of spirit' (line 12).

266. of such misery. As the line stands, 'misery' must be read with the stress accent on the second syllable. But there is doubtless a monosyllable, such as 'slow' or 'sad', dropped out, by printer's error, after 'such'.

269. Observe the beautiful rhythm in this monosyllabic line.

271. a love, used of a friend here, as in iii. 4. 7, 13, 17.

277. Which, referring to 'a wife'. 'Which' was often applied to persons (as 'who' to things) in Tudor English, cf.:

> " The mistress which I serve ", *Tempest*, iii. 1. 6.
> (*Abbott*, § 265.)

280. Bassanio is not to be taken literally in his readiness to sacrifice his wife. He is expressing his feelings with exaggerated force. The passage amuses the audience in the theatre, who have almost forgotten Portia in the Judge, and have been moved by the sad reality of Antonio's farewell. The situation is full of 'irony', but the irony is comic, not tragic. Gratiano and Nerissa extend the relief for a moment longer.

292. pursue, accented on the *first* syllable.

298. A sentence! Come, prepare! Here, as Irving acts the
part, Shylock makes a spring at Antonio, in front of whom Bassanio
flings himself.

300. This bond doth give thee here no jot of blood.
Portia's judgment has given rise to great controversy among the
critics. A full account of the controversy is given in Furness'
Variorum Edition.

It must be remembered that Shakespeare did not *invent* the
judgment, but took it from the old story in *Il Pecorone.*

It has been pointed out that Portia's interpretation overlooks the
general understanding "that the right to do a certain act confers the
right to the necessary incidents of that act", *e.g.* that the right to cut
a piece off a melon, confers the right to spill some of its juice.

But to appeal to such a general understanding is to appeal to a
principle of common sense or equity, which is not 'nominated in the
bond'; therefore Shylock has no more right to invoke it, than Portia
had a right to compel him to provide a surgeon for Antonio at his
own cost.

The judgment is an ancient and traditional one, and is far indeed
from being a mere quibble. It belongs to an exceedingly important
class of decisions, by which, under the guise of extreme severity,
equity was introduced into law, without injury to its stability. Such
judgments struck the common imagination deeply because of the
cleverness with which the law was saved from defeating its own purpose, and causing injustice. The judgment of Solomon is one instance;
another is that of the judge who, being called upon to punish a man
for having killed a youth's father by accidentally falling from a high
window upon him, bade the youth go and fall out of the same
window on the defendant—a means of redress which the youth
naturally declined to **accept.**

In later times such decisions became 'bad law', merely because
law had absorbed so much of the spirit of equity.

[In connection with the notes on lines 86 and 200 above, as to
the similarity of Shylock's position to that of the Pharisees, it is
interesting to remember that St. Paul's refutation of the 'Judaizers'
of his time was, in essence, the same as that of the judgment here.
If the letter of the law is to be invoked, it must be invoked in every
detail and in every particular ("thou art a debtor to the whole law"),
which is seen immediately to be impracticable, since no man *can*
keep it with absolute precision. The new 'spirit', however, does
not defeat or subvert the law, it fulfils it and completes it, and so
saves the law itself from self-destruction.]

Shakespeare is careful to add to the old solution a further point of
his own ("the law has yet another hold"), viz., that the bond was
an alien's attempt to murder a citizen, and therefore, *ipso facto,*
criminal.

325. estimation, *i.e.* on the scales, 'weight'.

328. on the hip. See note on i. 3. 40.

329. Why doth the Jew pause? He is hesitating whether to choose his revenge or his life, unconscious that, should he still resolve to take his pound of flesh, the young judge had 'another hold on him'.

336. barely. Note the effectiveness of the metrical form here.

340. stay question, as above, ii. 8. 40, 'stay the riping of the time', where 'stay' = 'wait for', and compare the colloquialism to 'stop supper' (Dickens, *Pickwick Papers*, ch. xxvi.).

347. seize, legal term = take lawful possession of.

367. Ay, for the state, not for Antonio, seems to mean that the half which is forfeited to Antonio *must* become his, while the court has power to commute the state's half for a fine.

374. There is some little difficulty in following the disposition made by Antonio. But the difficulty is lessened by reading a comma, as in the text, instead of a semicolon, as in the 'Globe' edition, after 'content'. The words then appear to mean: 'If it please the court to remit the fine in respect of that half of his goods which is due to the state, I am content to give the other half,—if I may in the meantime have the use of it as capital,—on Shylock's death, to Jessica and her husband'. Thus Shylock would keep one half of his goods, while Antonio would trade with the other half during Shylock's lifetime. At his death, the sum-total of his property would pass to Lorenzo and Jessica.

390. I am not well. This passage, with the lines 367–371 above, excites our pity for Shylock. He goes out. We hear the crowd howl at him at the door of the court, and then he disappears from our knowledge. We know, however, that he signed the deed in favour of Lorenzo and Jessica (see Act v. 1. 265). But what became of him? Each of us may have his idea. It would make a good subject for an essay or 'study'. That his treatment would seem merciful in Shakespeare's time, there can be no doubt. That Shakespeare himself approved of it, we have no evidence to show. On the stage, great actors like Kean and Irving have taken it for granted that we are to pity him, and have made his exit miserably sad to see.

392. The twelve godfathers are the twelve jurymen. Such a reference to purely English institutions is of a piece with the mention of a 'charter' in the case of Venice. See note on iii. 2. 276.

395. I entreat you home, verb of motion implied, as above, 'Father, in', ii. 2. 141, and line 397 below, 'I must away'.

396 contains another obsolete use of the preposition 'of' to be added to a collection of such in this play. See also 'of force' in line 415 below.

398. presently = immediately, as above, 381, and ii. 6. 65; ii. 9. 3.

400. gratify, thank and reward.

405. three thousand ducats. The payment of a fee by the winning side to a judge or referee seems, to modern ideas, a dangerous form of corruption, but it was quite regular in old days. Here the Duke himself recommends a reward of some kind. See further J. T. Doyle's note in Furness' Variorum Edition, p. 417.

415. of force I must, I am necessarily obliged.

425. to give you this, *i.e.* by giving you this. So in i. 1. 126, 'make moan *to* be abridged', means '*at* being abridged'. Abbott, *Shakesp. Gr.*, § 356.

426. methinks. In this phrase 'thinks' is an impersonal verb meaning 'seems', while 'me' is dative case.

439. An if. This 'an' is the conjunction 'and', as it is often spelt. For an explanation of the use, see Abbott, *Shakesp. Gr.*, §§ 101–103.

445. commandment is to be pronounced as a quadrisyllable. It is written 'commandement' in the First Folio. Abbott compares *1 Henry VI.*, i. 3. 20, "From him I have express command(e)ment".

Scene 2.

More of the adventure of the rings.

6. upon more advice, after more thought. So 'advised'= careful, thoughtful, i. 1. 140, &c.

16. old swearing, 'old' is used in its familiar, jocular application (as in such phrases as 'old boy', 'old girl', &c.)—not confined to schoolboys in Shakespeare's time. So Sir Thomas North, in translating the *Life of Alexander the Great*, writes "At this feast there was *old* drinking". Cp. also *Macbeth*, ii. 3. 2, and *Much Ado*, v. 2. 98.

Act V.

Of the home-coming of Portia and Bassanio; how he brings the Merchant with him from Venice; and of the end of the adventure of the rings.

The scene is the avenue to Portia's house. Around is the garden, "full of tall shrubs and lofty trees,—the tulip tree, the poplar, and the cedar. There are terraces and flights of steps, cascades and fountains, broad walks, avenues, and ridings, with alcoves and banqueting-houses in the rich architecture of Venice."

Lorenzo and Jessica are waiting for the return of their friends. The interval is filled with talk that richly interprets "soft stillness and the night", and with music played by Portia's musicians "of the house".

Shakespeare does not usually end a play—in the modern fashion—on its culminating sensation, nor send his audience away with their heart in their mouth. He winds his threads of story quietly off. (See the close, for instances, of *Hamlet* and of *Romeo and Juliet*.)

He adds here a consummately beautiful picture of tranquillity and happiness, necessary to restore the balance of the comedy, after the anguish of the trial scene.

1. **In such a night.** These miniature pictures of three 'star-crossed lovers' and of the witch Medea embody the secrecy, the passion, and the sadness of a moonlit night.

The detail of the pictures is Shakespeare's own, but the persons, as Hunter shows, were probably suggested to him by Chaucer's *Troilus and Cressida* and *Legend of Good Women*, in the latter of which Thisbe, Dido, and Medea follow one another.

10. **stood Dido.** This is perhaps the most beautiful of the series of pictures. Whether or no Shakespeare read Virgil, he was fond of Dido, and several times refers to her. He believed she was reconciled to Æneas in the after-world:

"Dido and her Æneas shall want troops
    And all the haunt be ours" (*Ant. and Cleop.*, iv. 14. 53).

willow, the token of unrequited or forsaken love.

12. **Medea gather'd.** The description of the herbs and other charms with which Medea renewed the youth of Æson, the old father of Jason, is to be found in Ovid, *Metamorphoses*, book vii.:

"Addidit exceptas *Lunæ de nocte* pruinas", &c.

Lichas, Midas, Hercules' rescue of Hesione, Orpheus, all figure in the *Metamorphoses*. It seems as if Shakespeare had the book fresh in his mind when he wrote the *Merchant*.

22. **outnight,** like 'outface' in iv. 2. 17.

28. **Stephano:** to be pronounced here with the *a* long. In the *Tempest* it is pronounced correctly, with the *a* short.

31. **by holy crosses,** such as are still to be seen in Roman Catholic countries by the roadside.

46. **post,** *i.e.* a messenger, so called from the 'posts' or stations fixed at regular intervals along the main roads, where change of horses, &c., could be obtained.

49. **Sweet soul.** Printed, in defiance of reason and rhythm, as part of the clown's speech, by all the early editions. The correction was first made by Rowe. See Appendix on the Text.

56. **creep in:** 'in' for 'into', frequent in Shakespeare. Cf. *Richard III.*, i. 2. 261:

"But first I'll turn yon fellow *in* his grave".

57. **touches,** notes.

59. **patines,** small plates of gold in which the consecrated wafer or bread is presented to communicants.

60. According to ancient theories of astronomy, the planets and stars were fixed in eight concentric spheres which revolved about the earth, making, as they moved, the music of a perfect diapason.

There are numberless references in English poetry to this 'music of the spheres'. In this passage the conception is rather different: it is the stars themselves, not the spheres, that sing; and it is possible, as has been suggested, that Shakespeare had *Job*, xxxviii. 7 in his mind: "When the morning stars sang together and all the sons of God shouted for joy".

62. still quiring to the young-eyed cherubins. One of the most magical lines in Shakespeare. 'Young-eyed' may be illustrated from Sir Joshua Reynolds' famous picture of cherub-faces. The line recalls, in subject as in beauty, Horatio's farewell to Hamlet—

> " Good-night, sweet prince,
> And flights of angels sing thee to thy rest ".

65. close us in. Rowe's emendation for 'close in it', of Q 1 and Ff., and 'close it in' of Q 2. It is plain that the 'it' at the end of the line has confused the printers. The meaning, or the part of it that can be expressed in prose, is: Immortal souls thus are full of a music which we mortals, while we are so thickly clad in perishable clay, are not able to hear. 'Grossly' conveys the double idea of thickness and insensibility.

66. wake Diana, that is, rouse the moon, which has now gone behind a cloud, and is asleep, as it were. The scene is not meant to be flooded with clear moonlight throughout. See also line 92 below. Further on again there is an indication that the moon is shining once more. What is the indication?

73. Note the effectiveness of the metrical form here.

77. a mutual stand, a general halt, as if by agreement.

78. Both **savage** and **modest** have slightly different senses here from their modern use. 'Savage' means 'wild', as a wild rose is 'rose sauvage' in French. There is no implication of cruelty in the word. 'Modest', again, is not 'humble', but 'orderly' or 'docile'. The Shakespearean meanings are thus nearer to the original 'silvaticus' and 'modestus'.

79. the poet. Ovid, in *Metamorphoses*, books x. and xi., tells the tale of Orpheus. But there may very likely be a reference here to Virgil's account of the legend in the fourth book of the *Georgics*. What other references to Orpheus do you know of in Shakespeare? What in Milton?

80. drew, in the same sense as 'draw' above, line 68.

82. his, the old possessive form of 'it'. Compare line 61 above.

85. is fit for treasons. Like Cassius, the typical conspirator (*Julius Cæsar*, i. 2. 200 ff.), 'he hears no music'.

These lines are sometimes quoted—like many others of the poet's —as if they expressed Shakespeare's own opinion. But the words are *Lorenzo's*. "Let no such man be trusted", seems to have irritated the commentator Steevens: see his long note quoted in

Furness' Variorum Edition. Instances to the contrary might be cited: Sir Walter Scott, Dr. Johnson, Dean Hook, Dean Stanley; good men who could not distinguish one tune from another.

87. Erebus, the covered place, the under-world, 'dim region of dead corpses'.

88. Mark the music. *Enter Portia and Nerissa.*
Portia is still full of the strong emotions roused in her by the trial; on her way home she has talked with the hermit, and prayed at the wayside crosses. For a while her reflections are grave and serious. She stands above Jessica and Lorenzo, and talks softly to Nerissa, while the music plays.

98. Music of the house, that is, a band of musicians.

99. good without respect, *i.e.* without reference to circumstances.

107. Good things miss their final flavour of perfection unless they are well-timed. There is a play on the double sense of 'season'.

109. Endymion, who slept an eternal sleep on the side of Mount Latmus, kissed by the rays of the moon.

121. tucket, a note or strain on a trumpet. Ital. *toccatta.*

127. day with the Antipodes, that is, daylight during the night as well as the day.

130. a light wife, a fickle wife, punned here with 'light' the opposite of heavy; as in the foregoing line it is punned with 'light' in the sense of 'brightness'. Portia, as we have seen before, makes skilful use of puns at moments when her friends might feel constrained or embarrassed. Her play on 'bound', six lines below, is an admirable instance of the cleverness with which she manages to be grateful without being formal or tiresome.

141. *i.e.* I cut short the politeness of mere words. For 'breathing', Malone compares 'mouth-honour, *breath*' from *Macbeth*, v. 3. 27. Compare also in this play ii. 9. 89, "commends and courteous *breath*".

147. cutler's poetry, the doggerel engraved on knife-blades.

154. respective, scrupulous, careful.

160. a little scrubbed boy, short or stunted like a scrub or shrub (two forms of the same word, cf. 'Wormwood *Scrubs*'). The comic 'irony' is delightful in this contemptuous description of Nerissa to her own self. 'A prating boy' ('plauderbube', as Schlegel turns it) is excellent from Gratiano, who had at last found someone that could outtalk him. Compare Lorenzo's complaint, i. 1. 106.

170-2. What difference do you note between the Shakespearean and the modern uses of 'leave' and 'masters' in these lines?

175. I were best, a confusion between two constructions:

(i) ' Me were best '=it would be best for me

[as 'you were best' in ii. 8. 33=it would be best for you],

and (ii) 'I had best'.

A different form of the same confusion occurs in *Richard II.*—

" *Me* rather *had* my heart might feel your love
      Than my unpleas'd eye see your courtesy " (iii. 3. 192, 193).

'I were best' is a case where the 'psychological subject', *i.e.* the person who is chief in the thought, has become, in spite of rule, the grammatical subject, chief in the grammar also. See Jespersen, *Progress in Language*, § 180, and Abbott, *Sh. Gr.*, § 230.

197. contain, keep.

199. much unreasonable, it is odd that we now only use 'much' in this adverbial way with adjectives of the comparative or superlative degree, *e.g.* 'much older', 'much the oldest', but not 'much old'. So, again, we say " I will come *very* likely", but not " I will come likely" (a Scotticism).

199–202. Portia, in her pretended anger, clips the connecting links between the clauses. 'Who is there so unreasonable (as to) have lacked good manners (to such an extent as) to press for a thing regarded by its owner as sacred?'

206. civil doctor, a doctor of civil law.

212. enforced, morally obliged; compare what Bassanio had said to the doctor—

" Dear sir, of *force* I must attempt you further " (iv. 1. 415).

213. beset with shame and courtesy, 'courtesy' the desire to show gratitude, 'shame' the desire not to seem ungrateful; the negative and positive poles of the same feeling.

216. candles of the night, stars, just as Banquo, in *Macbeth*, says of a cloudy night, " There's husbandry in heaven; their *candles* are all out ".

236. which, refers to 'body', not to 'wealth'.

239. advisedly, deliberately.

242. swear to keep this ring. Note, in point of dramatic construction, that the incident of the rings is not a mere 'excrescence' on the plot, but serves to bring about the recognition and explanation at the close with more spirit and humour than would have been possible by any other device.

249. as soon as you. See note at the beginning of Act iii. sc. 4.

251. Antonio, you are welcome. Portia has revealed herself now as Doctor Balthasar of Rome, and she welcomes Antonio once again in her double character.

Here is the crowning point of the play. The Merchant of Venice recognizes in the heroine of the caskets the heroine of the bond, his own deliverer in the wife of his dearest friend; here we learn that his ' argosies with portly sail ', in the fate of which we were interested at the opening of the play (i. I. 9), have come richly to harbour; here also the romance of the flight of the miser's daughter comes to a comfortable end; by Portia's care her future fortune is assured.

259. living = property, as in iii. 2. 158.

261. road, compare i. I. 19.

267. manna, one more reference to a Bible story. How many other such references can you recall from the play?

271. inter'gatories, a clipped form of 'interrogatories', questions which a witness was sworn to give true replies to; a phrase, as Lord Campbell tells us, that belongs to the Court of Queen's Bench. Portia speaks once more as the ' Civil Doctor '.

APPENDIX A.

THE TEXT.

Beginners in Shakespearean study need not concern themselves with minute questions of textual criticism, but it is
important they should know some preliminary points.

We have good reason for thinking that in many obscurely-
worded passages of Shakespeare, the obscurity arises from
the fact that we have not got the words as he wrote them.

Half his plays were not printed at all during his lifetime.
The other half show no traces of having been printed under
his supervision or with his correction.

The plays printed during his lifetime were printed singly
and in quarto size (called *quarto* because each page is of the
size of the *fourth* part of a full sheet of foolscap).   The first
collected edition of the plays was printed in 1623, seven
years after Shakespeare's death, and was edited by two fellow-
actors of his, Heminge and Condell.   This edition is known
as the First Folio (called *Folio* because each page has the
full length of a foolscap sheet or *leaf*).

The Merchant of Venice is one of the plays printed in
Shakespeare's lifetime.   Two Quarto editions of the play
appeared, both in 1600; one certainly, and the other almost
certainly, printed by J. Roberts.   The edition known as the
First Quarto was not only printed but also *published* by J.
Roberts.   The so-called Second Quarto was published by
Thomas Heyes.

The play was not printed again until it appeared in the
First Folio, 1623.[1]

Even nowadays when elementary schools, machine-print-
ing, and systematic revision of proofs have greatly reduced
the number of printers' errors, an editor finds much to correct
before a book can be published.   But in Shakespeare's time,
when spelling was so uncertain, when printing was often
done by ill-educated journeymen with insufficient type at

---

[1] These three editions are known to critics by the symbols Q^1, Q^2, F^1.

their own houses, when authors were indifferent as to how their plays appeared or whether they appeared at all, it is not wonderful to find editions full of mistakes in punctuation, spelling, grammar, and sense.

It might be thought, however, that where there are three early editions (as in the case of *The Merchant of Venice*) one would serve to correct another. In printing from manu-script, different printers would make different mistakes, but in each instance probably one at least would preserve the true version.

Unhappily this does not prove to be the fact. The three editions often contain in the same form what is manifestly a printer's blunder, *e.g.* in iii. 4. 49, 'Mantua' for 'Padua', and in ii. 7. 69, 'Gilded timber' for 'Gilded tombs', and in punctuation, ii. 7. 18, 'This casket threatens men that hazard all' for 'This casket threatens. Men that hazard all'. [See also Notes on ii. 1. 35; iv. 1. 50.]

These cases show that the three editions are really one edition. They are not independent sources from which we can derive a text by comparison, but are printed one from another. The variations which do occur (and there are hundreds of them, chiefly slight) are only so many more proofs of general inaccuracy.

Under these circumstances, Shakespearean scholars and editors have in many places had to exercise their own judg-ment in endeavouring to restore the words of the play as Shakespeare wrote them. Such an attempted restoration is called a '*conjectural emendation*'. The most famous of all Shakespearean emendations is one in the description of Falstaff's death in *Henry V.* where 'a table of green frieze' has been altered into ''a babbled of green fields'. This emendation is due to Theobald, who edited Shakespeare early in the eighteenth century. Other famous commentators on the text of Shakespeare are Rowe, Pope, Capell, Johnson, Steevens, Malone, Dyce, and Collier.

The emendations of these different scholars and critics, along with the readings of the early editions, are printed in the 'Cambridge' edition, and in Furness' 'Variorum' edition, so that the student has there the materials for making up his own mind as to what Shakespeare wrote in the disputed passages.

In this edition the text of the 'Globe'[1] edition, as reprinted

---

[1] Edited by Clark & Wright, the editors of the 'Cambridge' edition and the 'Clarendon Press' edition of Shakespeare.

in 1887, has been mainly followed. Necessary omissions have been made, and a few alterations, of which the chief are these :

- ii. 7. 40—Omit hyphen between 'mortal' and 'breathing', inserted first by Dyce. The curiously parallel phrase in *Richard III.*, iv. 4. 26, 'mortal living ghost', shows the hyphen to be unnecessary.

- iii. 2. 111—Print as one line, ' O love, be moderate, allay thy ecstasy'.

- iii. 2. 112—'rain thy joy' with the Ff., not 'rein' as in Globe ed.

- iii. 2. 163—'happier, then, in this' for 'happier than this' with F2, &c.

- iii. 2. 165[1]—'Happiest of all in' for 'Happiest of all is', with Collier, ed. 2.

- iii. 2. 201—Punctuate with Theobald. No stop at 'intermission'.

- iii. 2. 217—'Salanio' for 'Salerio', with Rowe, and so throughout.

- iii. 2. 317—Punctuate as suggested by Charles Kemble.

- iii. 3. 26, 28, 29—Punctuate and emend as suggested in Theobald's letter to Warburton (see *Furness*, p. 171).

- iii. 4. 53—'traject' for 'tranect' with Rowe.

- iii. 5. 52, 53—the reading 'meane it, it' of the Folios should be 'merit it', and 'Is' should be ''T is' (S. Walker).

- iv. 1. 125—'inexorable' with F3.

- iv. 1. 323—'Of' for 'Or' with Keightley.

- iv. 1. 376—Punctuate with Johnson.

- iv. 1. 383—'possess'd *of*' with Capell, as in v. 1. 266.

- v. 1. 65—'us in' for 'it in' with Rowe, ed. 2.

- v. 1. 167—Omit 'so' before 'riveted'. It has come in from the last line but one.

---

[1] As a proof that 'in' and 'is' are exchanged by printers even in a careful modern book, see p. 65 of the 1870 edition of Mrs. Jameson's *Characteristics of Women*, where—

> "which to term in gross
> Is an unlesson'd girl "

is printed—

> " which to term is gross
> Is an unlesson'd girl ".

For an amusing instance of a typical printer's error, see leading article in the *Daily News*, London, 24th December, 1896, where a phrase (used by Mr. Gladstone of book-collecting) "quirks and eccentricities" is quoted as "quicksand eccentricities".

APPENDIX B.

PROSODY.

1. **Metre and Rhythm.**—Fully to enjoy reading Shakespeare, whether to oneself or aloud, it is necessary to feel the effect of his use of *metre*.

Metre is one form of rhythm. The nature of *rhythm* may be understood by a comparison of dancing with walking. In walking, the movement comes, as we say, 'anyhow', without system or scheme. But in dancing there occurs from time to time among the steps a more emphatic step, made with a special *stress* or *beat* or *accent*. This accented step returns so regularly as to divide the movements of the dancer into groups occupying equal times. The motion thus becomes periodic, and the periods are marked by a pulsation, or recurrence of stress. Such periodicity is called *rhythm*. Alike in dance, in verse, and in music, rhythm is a necessary element.

Rhythm in uttered speech, if so precise as to be reducible to a formula or scheme, is called *metre*. Rhythm, of a less regular kind, is also found in prose, especially in oratorical prose. But metre is proper to verse only.

2. **Blank Verse.**—The metre used by Shakespeare for the main body of his plays is called Blank Verse. In this, rhythm is produced by an alternation of stressed and unstressed syllables, as in the word ago'. A pair of syllables, the second of which carries the metrical stress, is called an 'iambus', or an 'iambic foot'. If the stress falls on the first of the two syllables, the foot is said to be a 'trochee'. In Blank Verse the first are grouped in sets or 'lines' of five. A line of five iambic feet is called an 'iambic pentameter', *e.g.*—

> 'Tis nine' o'clock': our friends' all stay' for you'.
>
> No masque' to-night': the wind' is come' about'.

These are normal Blank Verse lines; or unrhymed Iambic Pentameters.

3. **Cautions to be observed in Reading Verse.**—It is to be carefully noted here that though the metrical stresses, as metrical, have all the same value, yet neither the above lines nor any others in Shakespeare are to be *read* with five equal stresses. The reason for this caution lies in the fact that

there is *emphasis* as well as metrical stress to be expressed, and that the amount of the emphasis depends on the importance of each word to the meaning of the sentence. Thus on the word "nine" there is not only a metrical stress equal to that on "clock", but also an emphasis of meaning which makes it necessary to utter the former much more forcibly than the latter. Similarly, the metrical accent on the last syllable of 'Jessica' may be the same as on the first, but the *accent of English pronunciation* puts a strong stress on the first and only a weak or secondary stress on the last.

Another equally important caution in reading is that the words must be grouped by their phrases, not divided at the ends of the feet. It is one of the chief beauties of good verse that the phrase-groups, into which the words fall, do not coincide with the metrical groups of feet and lines, but form, as it were, patterns of their own upon the pattern of the metre. It is in this counterplay between the metre and the sense that the charm of versification lies. From this it follows as a practical corollary that to read verse well one must so mark the rhythm as not to injure the sense, and so render the sense as not to spoil the rhythm. Thus the ends of the lines must always be indicated, but where there is no pause in the sense, the pause in the rhythm must be so brief as not to impair the continuity of the meaning. Similarly the metrical beat must always be rendered, but along with it the accent required by pronunciation and the emphasis demanded by the sense must be so clearly given as to prevent the 'sing-song' or 'see-saw' effect produced by reading lines simply according to their scansion. So also while, considered metrically, the time of all Blank Verse lines is equal, the metrical effect is not impaired by differences of time in actual reading, if, and so far as, these differences are accounted for by something in the thought or feeling expressed by the various lines.

4. **Prose Passages.**—More than one-fifth of *The Merchant of Venice* is written in prose. The transition from verse to prose or from prose to verse is often made within the limits of the same scene (*e.g.* i. 1. 112–120, i. 3. 1–33, &c. &c.). The principle on which the change is made is so subtle, that it does not admit of being formulated except in very general terms. It holds good that passages where the tone of the dialogue is light, and free from strong feeling, are usually in prose. Thus Launcelot never[1] speaks in blank verse, but

---

[1] As evidence that blank verse was felt to be unsuited to the expression of "casual" talk, see what Jaques says to Orlando when he changes to it from

F 3 (M 330)

(except for a few lines of rhymed doggerel) uses prose only. The confidential talk between Portia and her lady-in-waiting is in prose. In the second scene of Act ii., Bassanio's replies in blank verse to Launcelot's pieces of prose, give an impression of good-humoured Dignity talking to Impudence. On the other hand Shylock speaks in prose, not only in his meditations on matters of business (i. 3. 1–33), but also in his most passionate denunciations of Jessica and Antonio, and even in his great assertion of the human nature of Jews (iii. i.), while, in the Trial Scene, his speeches are entirely in Blank Verse. Perhaps we shall not be wrong in concluding that while blank verse was felt to be unsuitable to the talk of clowns or to familiar 'chat' of any kind, prose was used not only in these cases, but also for the sake of variety or contrast in passages of every mood of feeling. The reason for the transition will be found in the circumstances of each case, but often we can say no more than that the change is itself the object aimed at, and that therefore the same effect would have been produced by an alteration from prose to verse as is got by one from verse to prose.

5. Heroic Couplets.—Besides this introduction of Prose, other means are taken to vary the Blank Verse. Sometimes the lines are *rhymed* in ' couplets', called, to distinguish them from Lyric Metres, ' Heroic Couplets'. This device is used in *The Merchant of Venice* for two main purposes :—

(i) To mark the close of a scene or the exit of one of the dramatis personæ (ii. 6. 58, 59, and 67, 68). Here the rhyme has the effect, as it were, of the striking of a little bell.

(ii) To give point to an epigram or proverb, that 'clenches' an argument, or sums up a point of view. There is an excellent instance of this in ii. 9. 80, and following lines—

O these deliberate fools ! when they do choose,
They have the wisdom by their wit to lose.

To which Nerissa replies—

The ancient saying is no heresy,
Hanging and wiving goes by destiny.

In two notable places in iii. 2. there occur sequences of couplets, spoken first by Portia, second by Bassanio (108–113 and 140–149), where the effect of the musical chime is to enhance the strong emotions of relief and joy felt by both

prose, "Nay, then, God be wi' you, an you talk in blank verse," *As You Like It*, iv. 1. 31.

when the crisis is happily past. (See also the 'quatrain' of pentameter lines at the close of the same scene.)

6. **Decreasing use of Rhyme by Shakespeare.**—But Shakespeare used rhymed couplets less and less, the more experienced he grew, during the course of twenty-two years, in writing for the stage. In the earliest comedies, for instance in *Love's Labour's Lost*, there is so great a proportion of rhymed couplets to blank verse as to show that he was in doubt which of the two forms of metre was the more suited to drama. At this early period he was also writing poems, such as *Venus and Adonis*, which are rhymed throughout. As he gradually discarded rhyme in his plays, there came an alteration in the style of his blank verse. So vitally connected are these two changes that we can best understand them by treating them together. This treatment will also best enable us to realize some of the more obvious and measurable characteristics of the versification of *The Merchant of Venice*.

7. **Effects of Rhyming on the Style of Versification.**—The change, then, in metrical style in Shakespeare's plays, is a progressive relinquishment of rhyme and of those features in verse which are fostered by rhyming, particularly by rhyming in couplets.

How does Rhyming in Couplets affect Verse? Read, and listen to, these couplets by Pope, the great master of that form of metre—

> For forms of government let fools contest,
> Whate'er is best administer'd, is best :
> For moods of faith let graceless zealots fight,
> His can't be wrong, whose life is in the right ;
> In Faith and Hope the world will disagree,
> But all mankind's concern is Charity.

Here you will notice the effect of rhyme is threefold :—

i. By inducing the ear to listen for the close of the lines, and by making a couplet a whole in itself, Rhyme has a tendency

(*a*) To bring the sense-pauses to the end of the lines.

(*b*) To make final words important.

ii. By calling attention to the correspondence and echo between one line and another, Rhyme tends to regulate or formalize metre, *i.e.* by making one similarity prominent, it encourages others.

iii. Rhyme limits the possibilities of sentence-construction, and—by causing one line to answer another—favours a style of epigrammatic contrast.

It is natural, then, that in the earliest comedies, we should find, in connection with abundant use of rhyme, certain characteristics in the Blank Verse, which may be summed up as —an even and somewhat formal rhythm, almost exclusively iambic, with sense-pauses regularly placed at the end of lines.

8. The Blank Verse of "The Merchant of Venice" marked by Flexibility.—In *The Merchant of Venice*, written when Shakespeare had been at work some seven or eight years, we find certain changes in versification which give it greater flexibility and freedom. The structure of the sentence, as it were, outgrows and overlaps the metrical framework, wreathing and twining about it 'like a rose upon a trellis'.

9. Freer Treatment of the End of the Line. — These changes may thus be classified:—

(*a*) The sense-pauses are not so regularly placed at the ends of lines, but are distributed over different parts, and thus greater variety and greater continuity are given to the verse.

(*b*) An unaccented syllable occurs frequently at the end of the fifth foot in a line, so making the ending *double* or *feminine*, as it is technically called. Sometimes there are two such extra syllables, particularly in the case of proper names, *e.g.*—

> I would have stay'd till I had made you merry.
> To furnish thee to Belmont, to fair Portia.
> And I must freely have the half of anything.
> How doth that royal merchant, good Antonio?
> But who comes here? Lorenzo and his infidel?

By partly filling the line-pause, this device links the lines together.

(*c*) A similar effect, in linking the lines together, is produced by putting a lightly-accented monosyllable under the last metrical stress in a line, *e.g.*—

> In such a place, such sum or sums as are
> Express'd in the condition (i. 3. 136).

> 'A cur can lend three thousand ducats?' or
> Shall I bend low (i. 3. 112).

Shakespeare became increasingly fond of this device (see

Dowden, *Shakespeare Primer*, p. 41), but it is very rare in *The Merchant of Venice*.

10. **Varied Rhythm.**

(*a*) Trochees are commonly used, especially just after a pause or at the beginning of a line.

> Gao'ler, look' to him: tell' not me' of mer'cy.
> On'ly my blood' speaks' to you' in my veins'.
> Must give'—for what'? for lead'? ha'zard for lead'?
> Emp'ties itself', as doth' an in'land brook'.

The trochee produces a specially characteristic effect in the last foot in the line.

Have all | his ven | tures failed? | What, not ¦ one' hit? (iii. 2. 264).
I know' | the hand': | in faith' | 't is' a | fair' hand (ii. 4. 12).
At Grat' | ian' | o's lodg' | ing, some' | hour' hence (ii. 4. 26).
Did I' | deserve' | no more' | than' a | fool's' head? (ii. ix. 59).

When a trochee comes at the beginning of a line, and an extra syllable at the end, the character of the rhythm seems quite altered, *e.g.*—

> This' is the pent'-house un'der which' Loren'zo
> Sit', like his grand'sire, cut' in al'abas'ter ;

(which have just the rhythm of "Need'y knife-grind'er, whi'ther art' thou go'ing?")

(*b*) Syllables of equal emphatic value are placed together so that the effect of a *spondee* is produced (*i.e.* of a foot of two syllables equally accented)—

To my' | heart's' hope'! | Gold'; sil' | ver, and' | base lead' (ii. 9. 20).
The moon' | shines' bright': | in such a night as this (v. 1. 1).
And they' | did make' | no' noise' | in such a night (v. 1. 3).
Sit', Jess' | ica'. | Look' how the floor of heaven (v. 1. 58).
Did feign' that Or'pheus drew' trees', stones', and floods' (v. 1. 80).

Notice the particularly happy effect of this variation in the line—

> And, when I ope my lips, let no dog bark! (i. 1. 94).

(*c*) In cases where there is a sense-pause elsewhere than at the end of a line, the same advantage is taken of it to admit one or even two extra syllables. These extra syllables occupy part of the time mentally allotted to the pause, and are therefore said to be 'hypermetric' or outside the metre. But, like the feminine endings, they produce a subtle varia- tion on the character of the rhythm. The student should carefully collect for himself all instances of 'internal hyper- metric syllables'. Neglect of them may spoil reading. Here are some typical cases:—

My Lord' Bassan' | *io*, since' you | have found' | Anton' | *io* (i. 1. 69).

By be' | ing pee' | *vish*? I tell' | thee what', | Anto' | *nio* (i. 1. 86).

Exact' | the pen' | *alty*.

> Why, look' | you, how' | you storm' (1. 3. 127).

Which pries' | not' to | the inte' | rior, but', | like' | the mart' | *let*, (ii. 9. 28).

Without' | the stamp' | of mer' | *it*? Let none' | presume' (ii. 9. 39).

Were not' | derived' | corrupt' | *ly*, and' that | clear hon' | *our* (ii. 9. 42).

I lose' | your com' | *pany*: there'fore | forbear | awhile' (iii. 2. 3).

O love' | be mod' | *erate*; allay' | thy ec' | stasy' (iii. 2. 111).

How could' | he see' | to do' | *them*? Hav'ing | made one' (iii. 2. 124).

Fad'ing | in mus' | *ic*: that' the compar' | ison'

May stand' | more prop' | *er*, my eye' | shall be' | the stream' (iii. 2. 45-6).

To entrap' | the wis' | *est*, there'fore | thou gau' | dy gold' (iii. 2. 101).

Defy' the mat' | *ter*. How cheerst' | thou Jess' | ica'? (iii. 5. 45).

Such 'hypermetric syllables' are specially common where a line is divided between two speakers, because here the reader or hearer allows for a special pause. See the instance quoted above from i. 3., and compare with it—

To come' | again' | to Car' | thage.

> In such' | a night' (v. 1. 12).

(*d*) The above case of extra syllables before pauses, must be distinguished from instances where two syllables lightly and quickly pronounced are counted as occupying the time of one.

The prod' | igal Chris' | tian.   Jess' | ica', | my girl'.

The con' | tinent' | and sum' | mary of' | my for'tune.

E'ven in | the force' | and road' | of cas' | ualty'.

In such instances the light vowels should not be slurred or omitted in reading, for then the variety[1] in rhythm that

---

[1] This variety may be be used to convey a special effect, as in Tennyson's
   " Myriads of rivulets hurrying through the lawn ".

should be produced by them is lost. Moreover they occur
in cases where it is wholly impossible to omit them, *e.g.*—

All broken implements of a ruined house (*Timon of Athens*, iv. 2. 16),

where the third foot must be read either as a tribrach (three
unaccented syllables) or as an anapæst (two unaccented followed by one accented syllable); or perhaps the fourth foot
may be an anapæst.

The light pronunciation of some vowels in Elizabethan
English makes it possible to understand how ' ocean ' can be
scanned as in i. 1. 8—

Your mind is tossing on | the oc' | ean',

or ' marriage' as in—

To woo a maid in way | of marr' | iage' (ii. 9. 13),

or ' interest' in—

And what of him? did he | take int' | erest'? (i. 3. 69).

compared with—

Was this inserted to | make in' | terest good' | (i. 3. 84).

or Portia in the two lines—

Her name is Portia ; nothing undervalued
To Cato's daughter, Brutus' Portia.

Similarly while ' Antonio' is in some cases scanned as a full
quadrisyllable, in others the last two syllables are to be
uttered so quickly as only to take the time of one. (Compare
i. 1. 73 with i. 1. 69.) Compare also—

With pur' | pose to' | be dressed' | in an' | opin' | ion (i. 1. 91)

with—

With this' | fool gudg' | eon, this' | opin' | ion' (i. 1. 102).

In like manner, the first two syllables of Gratiano only count
as taking the time of one in i. 1. 77, but in i. 1. 107 the word
is a full quadrisyllable.

The same word may even be differently ' timed' in different
places in the same line, *e.g.*—

A se' | cond Dan' | iel', | a Da' | niel, Jew' | (iv. 1. 327).
And so', | though yours', | not' yours : Prove' | it so' (iii. 2. 20).

The terminations -*sion*, and -*tion*, are often allowed the time of two syllables, *e.g.*—

> Before' | a friend' | of this' | descrip' | tion',
> You' loved, | I' loved, | for in' | termiss' | ion',

and in the words imposition, preparation, occasion, perfection, contemplation, and others in this play.

On the other hand they often have the time of only one syllable, *e.g.*—

> Hath come' | so near' | crea' | tion? Move' | these eyes'?
> Of this' | fair man' | sion, mas' | ter of' | my ser' | vants.

A few other cases of words timed in a manner different from modern usage may be quoted, *e.g.*—

> There is' | no pow' | er in' | the tongue' | of man' (iv. 1. 235).
> Shall lose' | a ha' | ir by' | Bassan' | io's fault' (iii. 2. 299).
> Do you' | desi' | re? Rest | you fair', | good sign' | ior (i. 3. 53).

Caution. At this point falls to be mentioned a point which requires careful attention. Neglect of it is a common cause of bad reading. The termination -*ed* has in Shakespeare very often the time of a full syllable, *e.g.*—

> The self-same way with more | advi' | sed watch'.
> The French' | and Eng' lish there' | miscar' | ried'.
> Can al' | ter a' | decree' | estab' | lished', &c. &c.

Failure to notice this ruins the metre of the line. Similar caution is needed to observe the old pronunciation 'com-man*de*ment', iv. 1. 451, and 'asp*é*ct', ii. 1. 8.

11. **Incomplete Lines.**

Certain other variations in the even flow of the Blank Verse arise from the fact that Shakespeare's words were written to be spoken, with action and gesture. Part of the time of a line may be filled by a significant pause, which has the value of a 'rest' in musical time, *e.g.*—

> As far | as Bel | mont.
>   — | In such | a night | (v. 1. 17)
> And ne'er | a true | one
>   — | In such | a night (v. i. 20).
> That she' | did give' | me — | whose po' | sy was' (v. 1. 146).
> I'll wait' | as long' | for you' | then.   — | Approach (ii. 6. 24).

Such pauses may sometimes be filled with a movement or

gesture.   For instance, when Bassanio is opening the leaden casket, we find the line divided between Portio and Bassanio—

> For fear | I sur | feit !
>   — | What find' | I here' ?

So when Morocco picks up the leaden casket to examine its inscription, we have the incomplete verse—

> What says this leaden casket ?

Salutes and bows may well fill up the time left by the short lines in i. 1. 65, and 72.   See also ii. 2. 158, 187; ii. 3. 9; ii. 4. 27, 6. 28, 9. 83, &c., where 'stage business' of some kind, such as the exit of a person or the drawing of a curtain, occupies the pause in the rhythm.   This helps us to understand why there are so many incomplete lines in Shakespeare's dramas, while there are none in a narrative poem like Milton's *Paradise Lost*.

12. Other Metres.

Other forms of metre besides the Iambic Pentameter occur in *The Merchant of Venice*, of which the chief are—

(*a*) *Anapæstic* (that is, a rhythm of which the characteristic foot consists of two unaccented followed by one accented syllable; as in Wordsworth's "At the corner of Wood Street, when daylight appears"), *e.g.*—

> Thanks, i' faith' | for si' | lence is on' | ly commend' | able (i. 1. 111).
> Whiles we shut' | the gates' | upon one' | wooer, ano' | ther knocks' | at the door' (i. 2. 116).

(*b*) *Alexandrine*, of six iambic feet, or Iambic Hexameter. This is found in the inscription on the three caskets,

> "Who choo' | seth me', | shall get' | as much' | as he' | deserves'",

and in odd lines, here and there, *e.g.*—

> Because you are not sad.   Now by two-headed Janus (i. 1. 50).
> To find the other forth ; and by adventuring both (i. 1. 143).
> What many men desire ! that many may be meant (ii. 9. 25).
> I will assume desert.   Give me a key for this (ii. 9. 51).
> Desired us to make stand.   His hour is almost past (ii. 6. 2).
> What, is Antonio here ?   Ready, so please your grace (iv. 1. 1).

In all these cases of single Alexandrines there is a pause almost in the middle of the line, and the second half seems to be finished with only casual reference to the first.

(c) Short *lyric* metres, as for the scrolls found within the caskets. These vary between lines of four trochees, the last of which is cut off at the accented syllable, *e.g.*—

> All' that | glis'ters | is' not | gold',
> Of'ten | have' you | heard' that | told'.
>
> There' will | come' a | Chris'tian | by'
> Will' be | worth' a | Jew'ess' | eye'.

and lines of four iambic feet—

> Your ans' | wer had' | not been' | inscrolled'.

The one song that occurs in the play, viz., "Tell me where is fancy bred", is composed in a similar way, of mingled iambic and trochaic lines.

APPENDIX C.

THE 'MEANING' OF THE PLAY.

The 'meaning' of a work of art is all that it suggests, whether of feeling or of thought, to those who study it. Its 'true meaning' is that which it has for a student perfectly fitted to enjoy and understand it. If the work of art be great and the student apt, the suggestions which it makes to him will be rich and manifold beyond his power of statement, and will keep on increasing in volume and in interest as his experience of life and of art becomes greater. Thus it is a commonplace to hear people say that the more they 'go through', the more they 'see in Shakespeare'. Even such a line as Antonio's—

> "Say how I loved you. Speak me fair in death",

though it is in words of one syllable, 'means' more to some than to others. So does the beautiful picture drawn in the lines in Act v.—

> "She doth stray about
> By holy crosses, where she kneels and prays
> For happy wedlock hours".

Still more is this true of the play as a whole. Its meaning lives and grows, nourishing, and nourished by, the rest of experience.

No formula or maxim or 'view of life' can be an adequate rendering of the meaning of a poem. At the best it can only give a part of its meaning, for the value of poetry, as of music and of painting, consists just in this, that it expresses by its special means what cannot be so well expressed in any other way. That part of the meaning of a poem which can be adequately rendered in prose is, therefore, just that part which is least characteristically poetic.

If this be realized, and if we further guard ourselves from the dangerous belief that the 'moral' which we disengage from the poetry is the core or central point round which the poet himself worked in composing the play, it will not be unsafe to try to state some ideas as conspicuously prominent in it.

1. **Love and friendship.**—Companionship, as the main thing in life, seems a vital part of the story of the play. It appears under the two main forms of friendship and love. Shakespeare does not, in word, distinguish the two, but speaks of Antonio as a 'true lover' of Bassanio (see iii. 4. 7; iv. 1. 271). With Antonio friendship is a pursuit, a fine art—

> "The dearest friend to me, the kindest man,
> The best-condition'd and unwearied spirit
> In doing courtesies, and one in whom
> The ancient Roman honour more appears
> Than any that draws breath in Italy ".

This heroic passion appears in another form in Portia. She also has, in this respect, something of the 'antique Roman' in her; and in spirit and loyalty does not fall short of "Cato's daughter, Brutus' Portia ". She loves Bassanio so truly that she 'loves' his 'honour more'. The sacrifice she makes in sending him off in an instant, at a time when there was every selfish motive for delay, becomes heroic from the gaiety and grace with which she covers the generosity of her sympathy. In the court of justice these two forms of companionship appear together. Antonio there offers the last proof of love, and is ready to give his life for his friend; Portia, with a brilliant activity not less moving than his dignified passiveness, rescues him by her wit and courage. The last act sets companionship in the richest frame of poetry and humour, and shows the very stars in harmony with it. In contrast to Antonio and Portia, with their troops of friends, stands the lonely figure of Shylock, who isolates himself from human kindness.

2. **Conflict between the letter and the spirit of law.**—Some

critics have seen in the play an illustration of two different
ways of treating law. According to these critics, Shylock
represents the Hebraic idea that right consists in the fulfilment of the letter of law. Thus when he says—

> " What judgement shall I dread, doing no wrong?"

he interprets 'wrong' to mean 'a violation of written enact-
ment'. So, too, he replies to Portia's saying, " Then *must*
the Jew be merciful" (by which she means 'he *ought* to be
merciful', or ' it would be better if he were merciful'), by " On
what compulsion *must* I ?" refusing to recognize any principle
but a legal one. And he sums up his case by declaring, " I
stand here for *law*".

On the other side Portia represents the idea of equity.
This does not mean laxity of interpretation. For instance,
she regards her father's will as completely binding upon herself, and refuses to tamper with it even to secure her dearest
wishes. So, again, she declines to 'wrest the law' against
Shylock, and declares that, for the sake of the state, contracts
must be upheld. Yet she so far represents the equitable interpretations, common in Roman law, that, by something not
unlike a legal fiction, she saves the spirit by pushing the letter
to extreme. As by the old maxim '*summum jus*' may be
'*summa injuria*', she restores the balance by an interpretation so rigid as to make execution impossible.

A pleasant example of the principle appears in her treatment of the compact between herself and Bassanio in the
matter of the ring. Here Bassanio directly breaks the letter
of his pledge. But he is true to its spirit. To believe that
Portia would be angry with him for giving the ring to the
saviour of Antonio would have been a case of the 'ugly
treason of mistrust'; it would have shown a doubt of her
good sense and temper. In this way, of course, she takes
his conduct, and it is easy to see under her pretended anger
that she likes him all the better for showing living confidence
instead of mechanical and formal adherence to the letter of
their compact.

3. The evil of usury.—Other critics have thought the play
to be meant as an attack on the practice of usury. There is
nothing, however, to show that any special stress is laid on
this point by Shakespeare. Antonio's principle that the loan
of money should never be made upon a 'business consideration' appears to rest on a confusion between two quite
different sorts of loans: (1) those made to ' a friend in need'.
(2) those made in the regular way of commercial transaction,

In early days of trade, when business was confined to a few people in each centre, there was practically no distinction between the two, and then the taking of usury seemed to be a mean advantage on a friend's necessities. But afterwards, when commerce began to be international, and to be carried on in enormously greater volume, a 'money market' and a system of regular loans came to be an essential part of the machinery of trade. To confine financial transactions to a merchant's circle of personal friends would now be as inconvenient as it would be to abolish the system of public hotels and to leave all travellers to the chances of private hospitality. 'Friendly loans', as Polonius pointed out, are apt to turn out badly both for business and friendship.

4. **Different ways of using wealth.**—The German critic Gervinus regards the play as illustrating different ideas of the value of *wealth*. Thus Shylock pursues it for its own sake, or for the sake of the power which it gives him over other men. He ends not only by cutting himself off altogether from his kind, but by losing all his property, except such as is given back to him in pity by his enemies. Jessica, by a natural reaction, punishes the miserliness of her father by a childish wastefulness, flings his money about, and exchanges a valuable turquoise ring for a monkey. Antonio is magnificently generous in his use of wealth, regards as its chief value the power which it confers of helping a friend in need, and yet allows himself to appear so over-anxious that he comes in for the wise rebuke of the light-headed Gratiano—

> "You have too much respect upon the world,
> They lose it, that do buy it with much care".

Portia's wooers fail in the riddle of the caskets from a shallow view of the comparative values of things, and are taught by experience that "all that glisters is not gold", but that folly and death may lie under precious metals. Bassanio gives an instance of the most difficult kind of high-mindedness about money, frankness in accepting a loan or a gift. With Portia he represents the just view of wealth, that it is a mighty help to pleasurable living, and that for the sake of friends one cannot have too much of it (iii. 2. 156). Yet that it is simply not comparable to the really important things in life, such as friendship and love, for which it must be freely given and hazarded (iii. 2. 304).

There are many other views of the 'meaning' of the play, some of which it is good practice to try to work out for oneself, *e.g.* that it illustrates the contrast between the shows of things and their reality, Bassanio's speech over the caskets being taken as the 'key-note' to the whole play. These different interpretations show how much there is in the plays of Shakespeare, and that the 'morals' drawn from them are as various as those from life itself. But they all start from the assumption that he wrote 'with a purpose', in the narrow sense of the phrase, whereas it seems that 'the purpose of his playing' ought not to be defined otherwise than in Hamlet's description of it, "to hold the mirror up to nature".

GLOSSARY.

abode (ii. 6. 21), stay, or delay; not, as in modern use, the place of such stay.

accoutred (iii. 4. 63), arrayed. Der. from Old French *accoustrer*, of uncertain origin, but most probably from *custor*, secondary form of *custos*, in the special sense of a verger. Thus 'accoutre' would originally mean to array in ecclesiastical garments.

advised (i. 1. 142; ii. 1. 42, &c.), thoughtful, deliberate, careful. 'Advice' meant 'opinion', or 'thought', not necessarily 'counsel offered to another'. 'Advise' meant 'to reflect' as well as 'to offer an opinion' in Elizabethan English.

albeit (ii. vi. 27)=though it be the case that, notwithstanding. 'Al' is found by itself in Chaucer in the sense of 'although'.

amity (iii. 4. 3), friendship. Fr. *amitié*, Lat. *amicitia*.

an (ii. 4. 10, &c.) is another form of the copulative conjunction 'and', used conditionally, like the cognate word in Scandinavian dialect. 'An' was gradually differentiated in use from 'and', like 'to' from 'too'. When this conditional sense of 'and' became obscure and half-forgotten, the word was 'reduplicated' by the addition of 'if', in 'an if' or 'and if', *e.g.* Authorized Version of St. Matt., xxiv. 48. *Vide* Abbott, §§ 101, 102, 103.

anon (ii. 2. 105), in one moment, immediately; der. from 'on' and 'one'.

argosy (i. 1. 9; i. 3. 15), a merchant vessel. Skeat agrees with Clark and Wright in deriving the word from the name of Jason's famous ship, the *Argo*, rather than from *Ragosie*, a ship of Ragusa. But see the article in the *New English Dictionary*, ed. Dr. Murray, where evidence for the latter derivation is given.

bate (iii. 3. 32; iv. 1. 69), a shortened form of 'abate', meaning to 'beat down', or 'diminish'. Der. from *abattre*, which is French for the Low Lat. *ab-batuere*.

bechanced (i. 1. 38), participle of 'bechance', meaning 'to occur', 'befall'.

beholding (i. 3. 95). See note on the passage.

beshrew (ii. 6. 52, &c.), verb, to call plague upon something; often playfully used, as when Portia says to Bassanio, "Beshrew your eyes"=plague upon your eyes. Der. from 'shrew'= scolding, cutting, harmful.

betimes (iii. 1. 17), adverb, early. Der. from 'by', preposition, and 'time'. Formerly 'betime'. The 's' is added on the analogy of adverbs like 'whiles', 'needs', &c., where the possessive case is used adverbially. A similar false analogy has formed 'besides' for 'beside'.

149

bootless (iii. 3. 20), profitless. Der. from A.S. *bót* = profit, connected with the comparative *bet-ter*.

bottom (i. 1. 42), strictly the lower part of a ship, the hull below water-line; then, generally, a ship carrying cargo.

bound (i. 3. 15). See note on the passage.

catercousins (ii. 2. 117), friends, a familiar term answering to the modern 'chums'. The origin of the word is obscure, but it most probably means those who were related or connected, by being 'catered-for' together, table-mates, just as 'companion' means, by derivation, one who eats bread with another. The old derivation from *quatre* is almost certainly wrong. See the article in *New English Dictionary*, by Dr. Murray, who compares a passage from a translation of Terence (pubd. 1598), in which *inimicitia est inter eos* is rendered "They are not now cater cousins".

cerecloth (ii. 7. 51), literally, a waxed cloth used in the embalming of bodies; so, generally, a winding-sheet. Lat. *cera* = wax.

ceremony (v. 1. 202), a sacred symbol, regarded with special awe. For its use in this *concrete* sense, compare *Julius Cæsar*, i. 1. 70, "Disrobe the images, If you do find them deck'd with ceremonies".

cheer (iii. 2. 310), subst. = aspect, or expression, look, mien. Der. from Low Lat. *cara*, a face or countenance. From this original sense flow the meanings 'gladness', 'hospitality', 'fare', &c.

cheer (iii. 2. 235), verb = to encourage, comfort, bid welcome. Der. from above (iii. v. 45). 'How *cheerst* thou?' = how dost thou *fare*?

close (ii. 6. 47), adject., secret, concealing.

commodity (i. 1. 178), an article of commerce or merchandise, opposed to money, as goods to currency; compare: "Some tender *money* to me, Some offer me commodities to buy". — *Comedy of Errors*, iv. 3. 6.

complexion (iii. 1. 25), the temperament, or 'blend of humours', the disposition or natural bent. So in *Much Ado*, ii. 1. 305,' jealous complexion'. Compare its use in passage quoted from Howell, in the note on i. 1. 101. It occurs in its modern sense, i. 2. 113.

compromised (i. 3. 72), agreed, *i.e.* having come to terms.

conceit (i. 1. 92; iii. 4. 2, &c.). See note on iii. 4. 2.

condition (i. 2. 112), temper, disposition. So in Chaucer's *Knight's Tale*:

"He was so gentil of his condicioun
That thurghout al the court was his
renoun";

and compare 'best-condition'd', iii. 2. 291.

confiscate (iv. 1. 305), for confiscated, like 'consecrate' for 'consecrated', &c. The Latin termination expresses the participial force without addition of -ed. Abbott, § 342.

continent (iii. 2. 131), subst., that which holds or contains.

conveniency (iv. 1. 79), promptitude, suitable to circumstances.

convenient (iii. iv. 56), prompt for occasion.

cope (iv. 1. 406), verb, to requite or meet. (Compare 'recoup'.) Der. from Fr. *couper*.

counterfeit (iii. 2. 115), subst., an imitation or picture, without any sense of 'spurious' or 'fraudulent' as in modern uses. So the adject. the 'counterfeit presentment of two brothers' in *Hamlet*.

cozen (ii. 9. 38), verb, to cheat or defraud. Dr. Murray compares French *cousiner*, explained by Cotgrave (1611) "to clayme kindred for aduantage or particular ends". So that the word would mean 'to beguile under pretext of cousin-ship'. This derivation is, how-ever, far from certain.

crisped (iii. 2. 92), partic. of the verb 'to crisp', meaning to 'curl into short, stiff, wavy folds'. Der. from Lat. *crispare*, to crimp.

disabling (ii. 7. 30), verbal sub-stantive = disparagement, or lower-ing.

doit (i. 3. 130), subst., a small copper coin, worth the eighth of a 'stiver', formerly current in the Netherlands. The word itself is Dutch.

ducat (i. 3. 1, &c.), a gold coin, in use, formerly, in several coun-tries of Europe. It usually con-tained a weight of gold rather less than that of the modern half-sove-reign. Its name is derived from the *ducatus* or 'duchy' of Apulia, where it was first coined.

dulcet (iii. 2. 51), adj., sweet. Der. from Old French *doucet* or *dolcet*, formed with diminutive terminative *-et*, from *doux*, Lat. *dulcis*.

eaning-time (i. 3. 77), the lambing season. The old A.S. word *eánian*, 'to bring forth young', from which it is derived, is connected with 'eke', below.

eanling (i. 3. 73), a young lamb.

eke (iii. 2. 23), verb, to augment, increase. Cognate with Latin *augere*.

envious (*a*) (iii. 2. 280),
envy (*b*) (iv. 1. 123), subs., { (*a*) full of hate.
(*b*) hatred; nearer in meaning than the modern words to the Latin *in-vidiosus, invidia*, from which they are derived.

ergo (ii. 2. 50), conjunct. = there-fore, used by Launcelot Gobbo to show off his learning.

excrement (iii. 2. 87), hair; not derived from *excerno* in this sense, but from *excresco*, and so = out-growth. It appears in the sense of 'hair' also in *Comedy of Errors*, ii. 2. 79.

fall (i. 3. 78), verb, used transi-tively = to drop.

fear (ii. 1. 9), verb causative = to frighten; (iii. 2. 29) = to be anxious about, fear for. Cf. iii. 5. 2.

fill-horse (ii. 2. 100), a horse that works in shafts. 'Fill' is a dialectic form of 'thill', a shaft. Compare *Troilus and Cressida*, iii. 2. 48.

fond (ii. 9. 27; iii. 3. 9) = foolish. "*Fonned* (the older form of the word), the past part. of the verb *fonnen*, to act foolishly" (Skeat). Compare with the double sense of 'doting'.

fraught (ii. 8. 30), the past part. of an obsolete verb *frahten* = to lade a ship with cargo.

frutify (ii. 2. 120), a blunder of Launcelot Gobbo's, perhaps meant for 'fructify', in the sense of to bring forth fruit, or metaphori-cally, to discourse.

fulsome (i. 3. 76), adj., pro-ductive.

gaberdine (i. 3. 102, &c.), a loose outer gown or frock. The word comes through the Spanish from a Celtic origin, and is con-nected with 'cabin', and 'cape' or 'cope'; the idea of shelter or covering being common to all.

gaged (i. 1. 130), under pledge or obligation. 'Gage' and 'wage' are the same words (compare *guard* and *ward, guerre* and *war*), derived from Low Lat. *vadium*, or *wadium*, a pledge.

gear (i. 1. 110; ii. 11. 150); for this gear = for the nonce, for this occasion. 'Gear' means 'dress, harness, tackle'.

go to (i. 3. 105, &c.) has the same sense as the modern 'come, come'.

"'To' is still used adverbially in expressions such as 'heave to'. 'Go' did not, in Elizabethan English, necessarily imply motion *from*, but motion generally" (Abbott, § 185).

gormandise (ii. 5. 3), to eat greedily, like a gourmand or glutton. Derivation unknown.

gramercy (ii. 2. 108), many thanks. Fr. *grand merci*.

gratify (iv. 1. 400), to thank, reward.

gross (i. 3. 49, &c.), subst., total sum.

guarded (ii. 2. 139), ornamented with 'guards' or facings. Compare, "Rhymes are guards on wanton Cupid's hose" (*Love's Labour's Lost*, iv. 3. 58).

guiled (iii. 2. 97), full of guile, as disdain'd = full of disdain, in "jeering and disdain'd contempt" *1 Henry IV.*, i. 3. 183).

hovel-post (ii. 2. 60), a post or prop that sustains a hovel or shanty.

husbandry (iii. 4. 25), control or management of a house. A 'husband' is originally an inhabitant or master of a house, a householder. It thus answers to οἰκονόμος, and 'husbandry' to οἰκονομία, economy.

imposition (i. 2. 90; iii. 4. 33), a stated condition. In the second passage, it rather has the meaning of a 'task'.

intermission (iii. 2. 201), cessation, delay; compare "Cut short all intermission" (*Macbeth*, iv. 3. 232).

knap (iii. 1. 8), verb = gnaw, nibble; so used by Cotgrave (whose dictionary was published in 1611) to translate *ronger* ["to gnaw, knap, or nible off"].

lading (iii. 1. 3), subst., a cargo, or loading of a ship.

level (i. 2. 33), vb., to aim at, shoot at, and so, to guess at.

liberal (ii. 2. 168), free, careless in behaviour. See note on the place.

lieu (iv. 1. 404); in the phrase 'in lieu of' = 'in return for'. 'Lieu' is derived from *locus*, a place. ['Lieutenant', therefore, is a kind of *locum-tenens*.]

magnifico (iii. 2. 278), a grandee.

manage (iii. 4. 25), subst., means originally the 'handling' (from Lat. *manus*, a hand) or control of a horse; then 'management' in general.

marry (ii. 2. 35, &c.), interjection or expletive, from Marie or Mary.

martlet (ii. 9. 28), a diminutive of 'martin', which is a general name given to the Hirundinidæ, or birds of the swallow tribe.

moe (i. 1. 108). See note on the place.

moiety (iv. 1. 26), a half, a portion. Derived from the Latin *medietas*, through French *moitié*.

neat (i. 1. 112) comes from an old neuter substantive *neát*, meaning ox or cow.

needs (iii. 3. 14), adverb = necessarily. The final -*s* is an adverbial ending, "originally due to A.S. genitive cases in -*es*". (Skeat.)

nice (ii. 1. 14), adj., dainty, fastidious. Schmidt cites a passage that illustrates this one: "*nice* affections wavering stood", from *A Lover's Complaint*. Compare also "sharp occasions which lay *nice* manners by", *All's Well*, v. i. 15. Derived from Lat. *nescius*. See the curious article in Skeat's Dictionary.

notary (i. 3. 133), a writer or lawyer, who from the 'notes' furnished by his clients drew out contracts and deeds in legal form.

ostent (ii. 2. 179; ii. 8. 44), outward behaviour, manner, bearing.

pack (ii. 2. 9), to set out, to 'bundle off'; properly, to make one's things up for a journey.

pageant (i. 1. 11), a spectacle, a show, derived from the Latin *pagina*, in the sense of a "moveable scaffold, such as was used in the representation of the old mysteries". See the interesting article in Skeat's Dictionary.

parcel (i. 2. 93), a group or set, a 'parcel of wooers'. The word is a doublet of 'particle', and meant 'a small portion'. Now used only of a 'packet'. [For its use here we may compare "I think the English a *parcel* of brutes". Miss Burney, *Evelina*.]

parts (ii. 2. 165), qualities.

party-coloured(i. 3. 78),motley, dappled. Der. from *partie*, a part.

patch (ii. 5. 45), a name given to fools and jesters, from their 'motley' dress.

patines (v. 1. 59), a plate of metal for the bread in the Eucharist. Derived from Greek πατάνη.

peize (iii. 2. 22), to hold in a balance, to keep suspended, and so to delay. The word is a doublet of 'poise', and is derived, through French *peser*, from Latin *pensare*.

pent-house (ii. 6. 1), a shed projecting from a building. Reference to Skeat shows that the modern spelling of the word is due to false derivation. [Compare 'crayfish', 'sovereign', &c.] The word was formerly 'pentice', or 'appentice'; from Latin *appendicium*, an appendage or 'annexe'; it was mistakenly connected with French *pente*, a slope, and 'house', as if it meant 'a house with a sloping roof'.

pilled (i. 3. 75), another form of 'peeled'. "Jacob took him rods of green poplar, and pilled white strakes in them" (*Gen.* xxx. 37). The two verbs, 'peel', to strip off the skin (*pellis*), and 'pill', to strip or plunder (*pilare*), were confused with one another.

port (i. 1. 124, &c.), behaviour, deportment, bearing ('carriage' in a metaphorical sense). In iii. 2. 79, "magnificoes of greatest *port*", it means 'rank' or 'position'.

portly (i. 1. 9), stately in movement, majestic.

possessed (i. 3. 58; iv. 1. 35), informed. To 'possess' the mind with something is to fill or occupy it; so, by itself, 'possess' = instruct.

presently (iv. 1. 381, &c.), immediately.

prest (i. 1. 160), ready, prompt. Derived through French *prêt* (i.e. *prest*) from Latin *praesto*. Compare Prologue to Act IV. of *Pericles of Tyre*, line 45, "Prest for this blow".

quaint (iii. 4. 69); 'quaint lies', that is, lies carefully arranged or 'made up', 'artistic'. An examination of the passages cited by Schmidt will show that 'quaint' in Shakespeare means 'tasteful', 'trim', 'out of the common', but *not* (as now) 'queer' or 'grotesque'. Derived through old French *coint*, from Lat. *cognitus*.

quaintly (ii. 4. 6), tastefully, artistically.

quality = (i) style or manner (iii. 2. 6); (ii) manners or accomplishments (ii. 7. 33); (iii) virtue or faculty (iv. 1. 178).

quest (i. 1. 172), pursuit, enterprise.

racked (i. 1. 181), stretched to the uttermost.

reason (ii. 8. 27), verb, to talk, converse. Compare *Richard III.,*

ii. 3. 39, "You cannot *reason* almost with a man that looks not heavily".

redoubted (iii. 2. 88), feared, or formidable.

regreets (ii. 9. 88), greetings, salutations. The prefix *re-* has no force here, unless it is an intensive force. So the verb "regreet" simply=salute, in *Richard II.*, i. 3. 67.

rehearsed (iv. 1. 356), pronounced, proclaimed. Nowadays the word has become 'specialized', and is applied only to the preliminary practising of a musical or dramatic performance. By derivation it means ' to harrow over again'; so, metaphorically, to repeat.

remorse (iv. 1. 20), compassion. This is its usual sense in Shakespeare. Compare "the tears of soft remorse" (*King John*, iv. 3. 50).

respect (*a*) (i. 1. 74), consideration; (*b*) (ii. 2. 174), care, thoughtfulness; (*c*) (v. 1. 99), "nothing is good without respect", *i.e.* without reference to circumstances. Nothing is 'absolutely' good.

respective (v. 1. 154), careful of obligation, conscientious.

rib (ii. 7. 51), verb, to inclose as with ribs.

scant (ii. 1. 17; v. 1. 141), verb, to restrict, confine.

scrubbed (v. 1. 160); see note on the passage.

self (i. 1. 148), adject.=same. Compare the German *selber*.

sensible (*a*)=sensitive (ii. 8. 48); (*b*)=substantial, tangible (ii. 9. 88).

shrewd (iii. 2. 241), biting, cutting, painful. Compare the ballad phrase, "shrewd blows". The modern sense of the word may be paralleled from the metaphorical usage of 'keen', 'sharp', and 'acute'. For derivation see 'Beshrew', above.

shrive (i. 2. 113), to confess, in the sense in which a priest 'confesses' one who declares his faults.

sirrah (i. 2. 115, &c.), an extension of ' sir ', used in a familiar or contemptuous sense.

skipping (ii. 2. 170), lively, volatile.

slubber (ii. 8. 39), to do carelessly, to sully. [So *Othello*, i. 3. 227, "slubber the gloss of your new fortunes with this more stubborn expedition".] The word is Scandinavian in origin, and is connected with 'slop', 'slobber', 'slaver', &c.

sonties (ii. 2. 38), apparently for ' saints ', or 'sanctities'.

sooth (i. 1. 1, &c.), truth. The word is by origin the present part. of an old Teutonic verb 'As', meaning to be. ' Sooth ' thus= τὸ ὄν, fact or truth. See the interesting article in Skeat.

squander (i. 3. 18)=to scatter. Skeat quotes a good parallel from Dryden, *Annus Mirabilis*—

" All along the sea
They drive and *squander* the huge Belgian
fleet".

The word is connected in derivation with ' squirt ' and ' squall '.

stead (i. 3. 6), verb=help, benefit. Der. from the noun ' stead ' =position or place, and particularly from its use in the phrase, "to stand anyone in good *stead*".

stockish (v. 1. 81), like a stock or stump, wooden, hard.

stomach (iii. v. 62), appetite.

sufferance (i. 3. 100; iii. 1. 58), patience, endurance.

suit (ii. 2. 160), a petition. The word is from Lat. *secta*, a noun formed from *sequor*. The same original sense has developed differently in a ' suit' of clothes and a ' suite' of followers.

surfeit (i. 2. 5, &c.), verb, to suffer from excess.

thrift (i. 1. 175; i. 3. 80), profit, success; from the verb ' thrive '.

traject (iii. 4. 53), ferry.

troth (i. 2. 1), a variant or doublet of 'truth'. Both are derived from a Teutonic base, *trau* = I believe.

tucket (v. 1. 121), from Italian *toccata*, a note or flourish on a trumpet.

unbated (ii. 6. 11), undiminished. See 'Bate' above.

unthrift (v. 1. 16), adject., prodigal.

untread (ii. 6. 10), retrace.

usance (i. 3. 39), the practice of lending money at interest.

vail (i. 1. 28), verb, 'a headless form of avale'; from Fr. *avaler*, meaning 'to let drop' (the verb from which 'avalanche' is derived).

varnish'd (ii. 5. 32; ii. 9. 49), used in a metaphorical sense, in the first passage=masked, in the second=decked out, adorned.

vasty (ii. 7. 41), adj., conveying the two ideas of 'immense' and 'desolate'.

very (iii. 2. 221), adject.=true.

via (ii. 2. 9), interject.=away!

whiles (i. 2. 116), conjunc.= during the time that. 'Whiles', like 'needs', 'twice', &c., is an adv. formed by adding the possessive suffix. In 'whilst', the *-t* is an excrescence of later addition.

wis. "I wis", in ii. 9. 68, should be written 'ywis', an adverb meaning 'certainly', corresponding to the German *gewiss*. The spelling 'I wis' is due to false derivation. See 'pent-house' above.

withal (iii. 4. 72), adverb; (iv. 1. 406), preposition. Derived from the A.S. phrase *mid ealle*, or *mid eallum*, which is used to emphasize a preceding noun governed by mid. 'Withal' is thus adverbial by nature. When used as a preposition it always follows its noun, and has the meaning of 'with'. (See Messrs. Clark and Wright's note, in the Clarendon Press edition of the play, on iv. 1. 408).

younker (ii. 6. 14), a young gentleman. The word is derived from the Low German *jonkheer*, or *jungheer*, which is the same as High German *junger Herr*, a young master, a gentleman.

INDEX OF WORDS.

GENERAL INDEX.

SHAKESPEARE'S STAGE IN ITS BEARING UPON HIS DRAMA

§ 1. The structure and arrangements of the Elizabethan theatre are still under discussion, and many points of detail remain unsettled. A very extensive and highly technical literature on the subject is available, chiefly in England, America, and Germany. It is based especially on the new evidence derived from (1) the original stage directions, (2) contemporary illustrations and descriptions. The following summary gives the conclusions which at present appear most reasonable, neglecting much speculative matter of great interest.

§ 2. When Shakespeare arrived in London, soon after 1585, theatrical exhibitions were given there in (1) public theatres, (2) private theatres, (3) the halls of the royal palaces, and of the Inns of Court.

Of the 'public' theatres there were at least three: The Theater, the Curtain, both in Shoreditch, and Newington Butts on the Bankside or Southwark shore. About 1587, the Rose, also on the Bankside, was added. All these were occasionally used by Shakespeare's company before 1599, when their headquarters became the newly built Globe, likewise on the Bankside. Of the 'private' theatres the principal, and the oldest, was the Blackfriar, on the site of the present *Times* office. It was also the property of the company in which Shakespeare acquired a share, but being let out during practically his whole career, does not count in the present connexion. At court, on the other hand, his company played repeatedly. But his plays were written for the 'public' theatre, and this alone had any influence in his stage-craft.

§ 3. The 'public' theatre differed from the other two types chiefly in being (1) dependent on daylight, (2) open overhead, and (3) partially seatless; and from the court-stages also, in (4) not using painted scenes. While they, again, had the rectangular form, the typical 'public' theatre was a round or octagonal edifice, modelled partly on the inn-yards where companies of players had been accustomed to perform, prior to the inhibition of 1574, on movable stages; partly on the arenas used for bear-baiting and cock-fighting;—sports still carried on in the 'theatres', and in part dictating their arrangements.

The circular inner area, known thence as the 'cock-pit', or 'pit', had accordingly no seats; admission to it cost one penny (6d. in modern money), and the throng of standing spectators were known as the 'groundlings'. More expensive places (up to 2s. 6d.) with seats, were provided in tiers of galleries which ran round the area, one above the other, as in modern theatres; the uppermost being covered with a thatched roof.

§ 4. **The Stage** (using the term to describe the entire scenic apparatus of the theatre) included (1) the *outer stage*, a rectangular platform (as much as 42 feet wide in the largest examples) projecting into the circular area, from the back wall, and thus surrounded by 'groundlings' on three sides. Above it were a thatched roof and hangings but no side or front curtains. In the floor was a trap-door by which ghosts and others ascended or descended. At the back were (2) two projecting wings, each with a door opening obliquely on to the stage, the *recess* between them, of uncertain shape and extent, forming a kind of inner stage. Above this was (3) an upper room or rooms, which included the actors' 'tiring house', with a window or

i

windows opening on to (4) a *balcony* or gallery from which was hung (5) a *curtain*, by means of which the inner recess could be concealed or disclosed.

§ 5. The most important divergence of this type of structure from that of our theatres is in the relation between the outer stage and the auditorium. In the modern theatre the play is treated as a picture, framed in the proscenium arch, seen by the audience like any other picture from the front only, and shut off from their view at any desired moment by letting fall the curtain. An immediate consequence of this was that a scene (or act) could terminate only in one of two ways. Either the persons concerned in it walked, or were carried, off the stage; or a change of place and circumstances was *supposed* without their leaving it. Both these methods were used. The first was necessary only at the close of the play. For this reason an Elizabethan play rarely ends on a *climax* such as the close of Ibsen's *Ghosts*; the overpowering effect of which would be gravely diminished if, instead of the curtain falling upon Osvald's helpless cry for " the sun ", he and his mother had to walk off the stage. Marlowe's *Faustus* ends with a real climax, because the catastrophe *ipso facto* leaves the stage clear. But the close of even the most overwhelming final scenes of Shakespeare is relatively quiet, or even, as in *Macbeth*, a little tame. The concluding lines often provide a motive for the (compulsory) clearing of the stage.

In the *Tragedies*, the dead body of the hero has usually to be borne ceremoniously away, followed by the rest; so Aufidius in *Coriolanus*: "Help, three o' the chiefest soldiers: I'll be one". Similarly in *Hamlet* and *King Lear*. In *Othello*, Desdemona's bed was apparently in the curtained recess, and at the close the curtains were drawn upon the two bodies, instead of their being as usual borne away.

The close of the *Histories* often resembles the dispersing of an informal council after a declaration of policy by the principal person; thus *Richard II*. closes with Bolingbroke's announcement of the penance he proposes to pay for Richard's death; *Henry IV*. with his orders for the campaign against Northumberland and Glendower; *King John* with Falconbridge's great assertion of English patriotism.

In the *Comedies*, the leading persons will often withdraw to explain to one another at leisure what the audience already knows (*Winter's Tale*, *Tempest*, *Merchant of Venice*), or to carry out the wedding rites (*As You Like It*, *Midsummer-Night's Dream*); or they strike up a measure and thus (as in *Much Ado*) naturally dance off the stage. Sometimes the chief persons have withdrawn before the close, leaving some minor character—Puck (*Midsummer-Night's Dream*) or the Clown (*Twelfth Night*)—to wind up the whole with a snatch of song, and then retire himself.

§ 6. But the most important result of the exposed stage was that it placed strict limit upon dramatic illusion, and thus compelled the resort, for most purposes, to conventions resting on symbolism, suggestion, or make-believe. It was only in dress that anything like simulation could be attempted; and here the Elizabethan companies, as is well known, were lavish in the extreme. Painted scenes, on the other hand, even had they been available, would have been idle or worse, when perhaps a third of the audience would see, behind the actors, not the scenes but the people in the opposite gallery, or the gallants seated on the stage. Especially where complex and crowded actions were introduced, the most beggarly symbolic suggestion was cheerfully accepted. Jonson, in the spirit of classical realism, would

have tabooed all such intractable matter; and he scoffed, in his
famous Prologue, at the " three rusty swords " whose clashing had
to do duty for " York and Lancaster's long jars ". Shakespeare's
realism was never of this literal kind, but in bringing Agincourt upon
the stage of the newly built Globe in the following year (1599) he
showed himself so far sensitive to criticisms of this type that he
expressly appealed to the audience's imagination—" eke out our
imperfections with your thoughts "—consenting, moreover, to assist
them by the splendid descriptive passages interposed between the Acts.

It is probable that the Elizabethan popular audience did not need
any such appeal. It had no experience of elaborate ' realism ' on the
stage; the rude movable stages on which the earliest dramas had been
played compelled an ideal treatment of *space* and a symbolic treatment of *properties*; and this tradition, though slowly giving way, was
still paramount throughout Shakespeare's career. Thus every audience
accepted as a matter of course (1) the representation of *distant* things
or places simultaneously on the stage. Sidney, in 1580, had ridiculed
the Romantic plays of his time with " Asia of one side and Africa of
the other ", indicated by labels. But Shakespeare in 1593-4 could
still represent the tents of Richard III. and Richmond within a few
yards of one another, and the Ghosts speaking alternately to each.
Every audience accepted (2) the presence on the stage, in full view of
the audience, of accessories irrelevant to the scene in course of performance. A property requisite for one set of scenes, but out of place
in another, could be simply ignored while the latter were in progress;
just as the modern audience sees, but never reckons into the scenery,
the footlights and the prompter's box. Large, movable objects, such
as beds or chairs, were no doubt often brought in when needed; but
no one was disturbed if they remained during an intervening scene
in which they were out of place. And " properties either difficult to
move, like a well, or so small as to be unobtrusive, were habitually
left on the stage as long as they were wanted, whatever scenes inter-
vened " (Reynolds).

Thus in Jonson's *The Case is Altered* (an early play, not yet reflecting his
characteristic technique), Jaques, in III. 2, hides his gold in the earth and covers
it with a heap of dung to avoid suspicion. In IV. 4, he removes the dung to assure
himself that the gold is still there. The intervening scenes represent rooms in
Ferneze's palace, and Juniper's shop; but the heap of dung doubtless remained
on the stage all the time. Similarly in Peele's *David and Bethsabe*, the spring in
which Bethsabe bathes; and in his *Old Wives' Tale*, ' a study ' and a ' cross ',
which belong to unconnected parts of the action.

It follows from this that the *supposed locality of a scene could be
changed* without any change in the properties on the stage, or even of
the persons. What happened was merely that some properties which
previously had no dramatic relevance, suddenly acquired it, and *vice
versa*; that a tree, for instance, hitherto only a stage property out of
use, became a *tree* and signified probably, a wood. The change of
scene may take place without any break in the dialogue, and be only
marked by the occurrence of allusions of a different tenor.

Thus in *Doctor Faustus*, at v. 1106 f., Faustus is in " a fair and pleasant green ", on his way from the Emperor's Court at Wittenberg; at v. 1143 f., he is back in his house there. In *Romeo and Juliet*, I. 4. 5, Romeo and his friends are at first in the street; at I. 4, 114, according to the Folio, " they march about the stage and serving-men come forth with their napkins "; in other words, we are now in Capulet's hall, and Capulet presently enters meeting his guests. This is conventionalized in modern editions.

§ 7. The Inner Stage.

An audience for which the limitations of the actual stage meant so little, might be expected to dispense readily with the concessions to realism implied in providing an actual inner chamber for scenes performed ' within ', and an actual gallery for those performed ' aloft '. And the importance and number of the former class of scenes have, in fact, been greatly exaggerated.

Applying modern usages to the semi-mediæval Elizabethan stage, Brandl (*Einleitung* to his revised edition of Schlegel's translation) and Brodmeier (Dissertation on the stage conditions of the Elizabethan drama), put forward the theory of the ' alternative ' scene; according to which the inner and the outer stage were used ' alternately ', a recurring scene, with elaborate properties, being arranged in the former, and merely curtained off while intervening scenes were played on the outer, or main stage. But while this theory is plausible, as applied to some of Shakespeare's plays (e.g. the intricate transitions between rooms at Belmont and piazzas at Venice, in the *Merchant*), it breaks down in others (e.g. *Cymbeline*, II. 2, 3; *Richard II.*, I. 3, 4), and especially in many plays by other dramatists.

It is probable that the use of the ' inner stage ' was in general restricted to two classes of scene : (1) where persons ' within ' formed an integral though subordinate part of a scene of which the main issue was decided on the outer stage; as with the play-scene in *Hamlet*, or where Ferdinand and Miranda are discovered playing chess in *The Tempest*; (2) where a scene, though engaging the whole interest, is supposed to occur in an inner chamber. Thus Desdemona's chamber, Prospero's cell, Timon's cave, Lear's hovel, the Capulet's tomb.

§ 8. The Balcony.

There is less doubt about the use of the balcony or gallery. This was in fact an extremely favourite resource, and its existence in part explains the abundance of serenade, ropeladder, and other upper-story scenes in Elizabethan drama.

From the balcony, or the window above it, Juliet discoursed with Romeo, and Sylvia with Proteus (*Two Gentlemen of Verona*, IV. 2); Richard III. addressed the London citizens, and the citizen of Angers the rival Kings. From the window the Pedant in *Taming of the Shrew*, V. 1, hails Petruchio and Grumio below; and Squire Tub, in Jonson's *Tale of a Tub*, I. 1, puts out his head in answer to the summons of Parson Hugh. But whole scenes were also, it is probable, occasionally enacted in this upper room. This is the most natural interpretation of the scenes in Juliet's chamber (IV. 3, 5). On the other hand, though the Senators in *Titus Andronicus*, I. 1, " go up into the ' Senate House ' ", it is probable that the debate later in the scene, on the main stage, is intended to be in the Senate-house by the convention described in § 6.

For further reference the following among others may be mentioned :

G. F. Reynolds, *Some Principles of Elizabethan Staging* (*Modern Philology*, II. III.); A. Brandl, *Introduction* to his edition of Schlegel's translation of Shakespeare; V. E. Albright, *The Shakespearian Stage* (New York); W. Archer, *The Elizabethan Stage* (*Quarterly Review*, 1908); W. J. Lawrence, *The Elizabethan Playhouse and other Studies* (1st and 2nd series); D. Figgis, *Shakespeare, a study*.

From one or other of these, many of the above examples have been taken.

C. H. H.